AFTER THE WAR

A MEMOIR

WENDY APPLETON

Contact: Wendy Appleton - flowerworld809@gmail.com

Cover design by CANDesigner

Editing and formatting by Debra Jones

ISBN: 978-1-7773155-0-4

First Edition: Aug 2020

With grateful thanks to all my family, and to my lovely, patient daughter, without whom this book would not have been published.

1

PICNICS AND JAM

I OPENED MY EYES TO THE SUN STREAMING THROUGH THE GAP IN the curtains. I could hear the silvery notes of a blackbird outside. He was sitting in the branches of the purple lilac tree near my bedroom window, and his little chest was puffed out as he sang his song for the entire world to hear. The sound of this little bird filled me with joy. Now that I was six and the war was over, it was so lovely to be woken by a bird singing instead of the cacophony of bombs falling, and anti-aircraft fire.

Turning, I looked at the small bed opposite mine. My nine-year-old brother Brian was still asleep, his thick brown tousled hair against his pillow and the old grey blanket tucked under his chin. I stretched my arms, yawned and climbed out of bed, my bare feet making no sound on the cold linoleum. I crossed to the window and pulled back the curtain. As I peeped out, the blackbird began his song again, opening his bright yellow beak wide; each note he sang was pure delight. Looking up at the pale blue sky, I watched as a few small puffy clouds drifted slowly towards the West. I knew it was the West because next door, Mr. Mepham's weather vane on top of his garage said so, as the cockerel on the top was facing that way.

Next door but one, I could see our neighbour, Mrs. Clayton's pretty blonde head bobbing up and down behind her washing line as she bent down to find a pillowcase to peg onto the line. She caught sight of me and waved. I smiled and waved back, then turned as I heard Brian moving. I had let too much light into the room while moving the curtain. He rubbed his eyes and squinted at me.

"What are you doing?" He asked as he climbed out of bed, "found some more bed bugs?" he added, grinning wickedly.

I pulled a face at the memory of the time I saw the horrid red beetles in my bed, and of the raised pink spots on my legs and arms. I shook my head, thankful that Daddy had finally got rid of those horrible creatures with the DDT puffer.

I sat on the bed, and as I began to pull on my socks, I remembered that today was the day Mummy had promised to take us blackberrying in the woods at Gravel Hill. I took my clothes and went downstairs to the bathroom to get washed and dressed. Mummy had been up early, making marmite sandwiches and packing empty jam jars into a large shopping bag. She added a bottle of homemade lemonade to quench our thirst. I loved Mummy's lemonade; it was sweet and sour at the same time. We would be filling the jars with blackberries ready to make the jam. It seemed the easiest way to carry the fruit, as I remembered from previous trips, berries could be a bit squashy.

I completed my ablutions and wandered into the living room where my one-year-old brother, Christopher was sucking on a rusk, small pieces of soggy bread stuck between his little fingers. I fetched a wet flannel and wiped them clean while he sat there smiling at me, then he put his fingers back in his mouth. I tickled him, making him giggle heartily, hugged him, plopping a kiss on his curls.

"You're my little cherub," I said.

"Cheb," he replied and chuckled.

Both Daddy and my elder sisters, Betty and Sheila, had left for work.

At breakfast, we all polished off our Kellogg's Wheat flakes quickly, and then Mummy asked Brian and me to do the dishes while my other sister, Thelma, helped her to get the boys ready.

"I want to wash," Brian insisted, grabbing the dishcloth.

"No, I want to wash," I replied.

"Well, if I can't wash, I am not wiping," he exclaimed.

I gave in, and picked up the tea towel. I knew he meant what he said, and I didn't want to have to do both jobs.

As soon as we were all ready, Mummy, Thelma, Brian, David, Christopher and myself set off. The sun was quite high in the sky now, and the chill wind had given way to a warmer breeze. Thelma pushed the pushchair carrying David and Christopher squashed in, side by side, while the rest of us trailed behind her, taking turns to carry the bag with the jam jars. Mummy was carrying a rolled-up blanket under her arm for us to sit on. We crossed over the Broadway and went down Highland Road. It seemed quicker to go that way, rather than traipsing down the Broadway until we reached the traffic lights at Gravel Hill. Turning left at the end of the road, we went another half a mile before finally coming to the countryside and further along, Gravel Hill.

Another half a mile or so and we found ourselves at the entrance to the field before the woods. It became difficult to push the pram on the grass, so, instead, we found a stony path that led us to the woods. The leaves were beginning to turn to their autumn colour. Some had even fallen off the trees. They made a swooshing noise as we ploughed through them until we came to a clearing between the trees. Here Mummy stopped and spread the Army blanket on the grass. She then made us all sit down and get our breath back as both Brian and I were feeling asthmatic and fighting for our breath by this time. Mummy was also quite breathless from the long walk.

Listening to the bird song and the rustling of the wind in the trees had a calming effect on me. I sat, propped up with my back against a tree, and looked around at the bushes and trees that surrounded us. The contrast of the rough bark next to the smooth leaves fascinated me. Everything was so beautiful. All was quiet except for the singing of the birds and the light breeze blowing through the trees. Mummy pointed to a bush near where we were sitting.

"Look at all those blackberries!" she said with a happy smile, "it looks like a good year for them," she continued, pleased that it seemed as though we were going to be able to harvest a fair amount of berries for her excellent blackberry jelly.

Thelma grabbed a jar from the bag and started to stuff it with large fat, black, juicy fruit, popping one or two into her mouth as well. Once we felt rested, Brian and I did the same.

While Mummy watched Christopher, I took David's hand and showed him the berries. As I picked them, thorns scratched my arms and hands and tore a hole in my cotton skirt, but I didn't notice, as I was so intent on filling my jar. We needed lots of the berries for Mummy's jam.

"If we find enough, I will make a pie as well," she said brightly, "I've got some cooking apples from Hancock's indoors, to go with them." The Hancock's owned the apple orchard in Woolwich Road. "Mmm, apple and blackberry pie!" Brian said, licking his lips, picturing it in his mind.

Meanwhile, David sat down on the grass and began popping berries into his mouth. I turned to look at him. There was a dark stain around his mouth, on his hands, and down the front of his little shirt.

"Oh, no! Look at him, Mum," I said, pointing to my small brother. His face began to pucker as he sensed he was in trouble. My mother smiled; nothing was going to spoil her day out.

"Oh, never mind," she said quietly, "it will wash off," she continued, although not altogether convinced that the dark stain would come out in the wash. "Maybe if I rub some salt on it," she said to herself as she gathered David up in her arms with a hug.

Finally, I had had enough of picking blackberries as my arms were beginning to feel sore from the scratches. I decided to look for fairies instead. I remembered that when we had come here earlier, there were several delicate, tiny pale blue harebells growing near the trees I had been sitting under, so I had knelt to pick one, peering inside to see the fairy that I was convinced lived there. I couldn't see one, so I shook the flower instead. It made a papery rustling sound, and I walked over to my mother and held it close to her ear.

"Listen," I whispered, shaking the small flower, "you can hear the bell ringing."

Mummy smiled as I skipped away to find some more flowers.

I didn't see any flowers, but I did find a fairy ring of little toadstools. I carefully lay down on the grass to see if there were any doors or windows in them, but I couldn't find any, and the fairies were also hiding.

It was a lovely outing; I did enjoy myself. It was wonderful to be in the countryside, free from all the noise and mayhem of the war at last. We no longer had to stay within walking (or running) distance of the nearest air raid shelter, always nervous in case another bombing raid put an end to whatever we had decided to do that day. On the contrary, we could now roam safely, and as far as we liked.

With all the jam jars now full to overflowing, we sat on the rough grass and ate our picnic of Marmite sandwiches and homemade lemonade, finishing with a biscuit and a handful of blackberries. Soon it was time to return home.

I had picked a bunch of twigs with berries and ferns, together with a giant toadstool and wrapped them in my hanky, to take home with us. I was secretly hoping that as I had their home, the fairies would come with us. I knew that they would hide from humans, so I would look away and then quickly turn my head again to see if I could catch them. It didn't work. But then, I reasoned, fairies could make themselves invisible, couldn't they?

The climb back up Gravel Hill seemed to last forever. I was so very weary and breathless by the time we had reached the top that Mummy stopped and made me sit in the pushchair with David on my lap, while she balanced Christopher on her hip. Brian, who was also puffing, hung onto the handle of the pushchair. Thelma pushed us slowly all the way home. When we reached the house, Thelma helped Mummy unpack the precious jars of blackberries, pouring them into a preserving pan. Brian and I watched, and then we washed the jars. Mummy put them carefully away in the larder, ready for jam-making the next day.

A delicious scent filled the house when Mummy made the jam. She stirred the dark fruit together with the chopped apples in her huge preserving pan, brought the liquid to a boil and then added the warmed sugar. Mummy then tested a little of the dark red juice to see if it had reached the setting point by pouring it onto a saucer. She would push her finger through the sample to see if it wrinkled, and if it did, this would indicate that the jam was almost set and ready to pot up. After skimming the white scum off the top of the jam in the pan, she filled each jar with the dark red boiling liquid. Thelma and I, in between licking the saucer, swatted the wasps that had flown in through the window, following the scent of the sweet preserves.

We both helped by placing the small circles of greaseproof paper on each jar, to seal out the air. Then we filled a saucer with water, placing the circles of cellophane in it so that when placed on the jars, they would stretch, producing a seal when fastened with elastic bands. When we were finished, Mummy surveyed the rows of jars with pride as she labelled each one with the name and date and placed them in a neat row on the shelves of the pantry. When Daddy came home from work, she showed them off, proud of the day's work.

Once Mummy had managed to buy some quinces to make some quince jelly. To separate the pips from the fruit, she placed the kitchen stool upside down in the bath, tied the boiled fruit into a large muslin bag, and attached it to the legs of the stool. She placed a pan underneath to catch the juice.

On the following Sunday at breakfast, our father announced with a big smile, "I am going to dig up the air raid shelter today; we shan't be needing that any more." How wonderful to be getting rid of it at last. It seemed to me that it had been there forever. I thought back to the many times we had crouched inside the cramped space. I remembered laying on my bunk, watching the condensation trickling down the walls, listening to the mayhem outside and wondering if the next bomb that dropped would be on us.

"Can I help you?" asked Brian. "You can all help me. Many hands make light work." Daddy replied.

I watched as my father removed the earth from the outside of the shelter, carefully saving the daffodil bulbs to be transplanted somewhere else. Soon, all that was left was the now musty corrugated shelter iron. With us all lending a hand, we lifted it out of the ground, and Daddy and Brian proceeded to fill the earth back into the hole that was left.

"Now we have somewhere to put the bikes and doll's pram," Daddy said with satisfaction, pleased that he had thought of a new use for the old Anderson shelter, it had undoubtedly served us well. How wonderful it was that we didn't need to shelter from the bombs anymore.

So now, the shelter was placed on top of the ground at the back of the shed. David's trolley, my dolls pram and the tricycle all had a new home.

My mother always insisted on taking us on an outing or two during the school holidays. Sometimes we would go to Gravel Hill, or Danson Park in Welling, or maybe to the vast Maritime Museum at Greenwich Park. The museum was established in

1937, so it was a little older than I, although the Palace that housed it had once been the home of King Henry Vlll.

In the Maritime Museum, I can remember staring into a glass display case at the pigtail of hair that had once belonged to Lord Nelson. In another room, was the unwrapped, mummified remains of an Egyptian mummy. It was dark brown and shiny, small and strange."Was that once a person?" I wondered, "They must have been very tiny people." I reasoned.

Afterwards, we roamed through the park, then up the hill to the Observatory, where we gazed at the glass cases of weird and wonderful contraptions. Outside we looked back down at the Palace; it was a handsome long white building, bordering the Thames River, surrounded by a beautiful park, full of Rhododendron bushes.

One day, Mummy decided we would go to Martin's Grove in Crayford. So Betty, Thelma, Brian, myself, David and Christopher, together with a picnic lunch and with our bathing costumes wrapped in towels tucked under our arms, started out to catch the bus by the clock tower. When we reached Martin's Grove, we all tumbled out of the bus. I looked around; we had reached a woodland area. We followed the path through the green trees. It was a large park with lots of trees, a woodland area, formal gardens, tennis courts and two outdoor swimming pools surrounded by iron railings; one pool for adults and the other smaller pool for the children.

We reached the pools and found ourselves a place to sit, while Mummy, with Betty's help, busily changed Christopher and David into their bathing trunks.

Then my sister Betty took me to the changing rooms by the adult pool, and we changed into our costumes.

"Come on," Betty said, taking hold of my arm. She loved to swim and decided that she could teach me.

So Betty took me with her into the adult's pool, she carried me into deeper and deeper water until my feet didn't touch the bottom, and then she let go, telling me to kick my legs and swim. Scared of the vast expanse of water and not knowing what to do, I began to sink and watched as the water closed over my head.

My active imagination recalled the memory of a story we were told about by the teacher. It was about a girl who drowned in the canal during the evacuation, and the vivid description of how she looked when found. As I came up spluttering and gasping, somebody grabbed me and carried me to the side of the pool. Betty got a good telling off, but she didn't think she had done anything wrong and couldn't understand why I hadn't started swimming. After all, it was so easy for her. She loved to swim and was very good at it.

We decided that I should return to the paddling pool – I could cope with that.

2

RABBIT PIE AND WILD FLOWERS

MONEY WAS VERY TIGHT DURING OUR SCHOOL YEARS, AND MANY times Brian and I had to take some of our old clothes to the 'rag and bone man' in exchange for a few coins to help buy some much-needed food. We would pile the garments on to the pushchair and take turns to push it, occasionally stopping to pick up garments that had fallen off.

Brian and I wandered through the back streets until we reached Mayplace Road, then crossing the road, we went down a lane opposite the Palace Cinema, between the shops. We found the rag and bone yard full of old iron, rusty metal and other exciting things. As we waited to have the clothes sorted and weighed, I stared at the old bicycles and strange rusty metal things that littered the place, wondering what possible use they could be.

"If we are lucky, he might give us half a crown," Brian said in anticipation, grinning at me. But this time we only went away with a florin. At home, we gave the precious coin to Mummy. "Only two shillings!" Our mother exclaimed.

Secretly she had hoped that by sending us instead of going herself, the man would be more generous. But it hadn't made any difference. I suppose he had to watch the pennies too.

Sometimes he would come along the road with his horse and cart shouting, "Any old iron." (At least I think that was what he was shouting; you never could quite make out what the actual words were.) People would come to their gates with old clothes and bric-a-brac to exchange for the much-needed money. On reflection, I am sure that it was always the rag and bone man who came off best in these transactions.

It was about this time that I remember Mummy and Daddy arguing about money (or rather the lack of it). Daddy's four pounds, ten shillings a week wages didn't go far to paying for Mummy's and our asthma medicine, and feeding and clothing seven children, not to mention paying the rent!

Things always seemed to come to a head at weekends when my parents would shout and yell at each other. I hated it, and one day when they were in the kitchen letting rip, I heard my father shout, "Now, don't get on your orange box!"

Mummy shouted back, "I'm not on my orange box! You…." Her words tapered off as I peeped round the kitchen door to see what was happening. Just as I did so, my father announced that he had had enough, and was leaving. Horrified, I yelled, "Can I come with you?" not wanting him to leave me behind. My mother turned on me; she was furious, "Oh, you *would* take his side," she hissed.

My face crumpled as I looked helplessly at them both.

"Now look what you have done!" My father shouted at Mummy, and stormed out of the house. "I'm going to the allotment!" he shouted over his shoulder (I think it was for my benefit.) I felt crushed and felt somehow it must be my fault that he had gone. Once more, I began to cry and ran upstairs to my bedroom.

Daddy had rented an allotment at the end of the road. A large part of the school field had been made over to allotments so that people had more space to grow vegetables. Even though the war was over, there were still food shortages, so we would always follow the wartime directive of "Dig for Victory!" With the lack of food in the shops, it made sense.

My father came back later when he had cooled off, carrying a bag full of freshly picked vegetables. I was so glad that he wasn't going to leave us after all.

Still, the arguments continued, and I can remember my eldest sister, Sheila, coming home on leave from the Land Army one weekend and accusing our parents of waiting until she came home so that they could fight. Sheila thought the fights were only at weekends. She didn't realize that Mummy and Daddy were at loggerheads through the week as well. I must admit things always seemed to come to a head at weekends when the lack of money was felt the most.

Despite the arguments, my father adored my mother, and she loved him too. They were worried about not being able to make ends meet. Mother's, Brian's and my asthma medication took a lot of the much-needed money, but my parents did their best to raise us. They did a fantastic job given what they had to work with, and regardless, we all felt loved and well looked after.

Sheila enjoyed her life in the Land Army, which was formed when all the men had to go to war, leaving the farmers without farm labour. They needed the women to plough the fields, pick the crops, look after the animals and milk the cows.

Sheila sometimes would bring us home a rabbit when she got leave to come home at weekends. When the wheat was harvested, the rabbits would dash out from their hiding places, and the farmer would pick them off with a shotgun.

Mummy would make the most delicious rabbit pie or stew with onions and carrots from the allotment. There was nothing quite like the taste of rabbit stew or pie. We would sing, the song made famous by Flanagan and Allen, the comedians we used to listen to on the wireless:

On the farm
Every Friday,
On the farm
It's rabbit pie day,
Run rabbit, run rabbit,
Run, run, run,
Don't give the farmer his
Fun, fun, fun,
He'll get by without his rabbit pie.
So run rabbit, run rabbit,
Run, run, and run!

After one of her weekend visits home, Sheila allowed me to go back to the farm with her . We travelled on the train through the Kent countryside. Sheila worked on a farm at Edenbridge, which was near Sevenoaks in Kent. She billeted (rented) with an elderly lady, Mrs. Watney. The old lady said I could come and stay there too.

Mrs. Watney lived alone and welcomed me like one of her family. I was allowed to roam wherever I liked and would wander along the country lanes while Sheila was working on the land. I would pick large bunches of wildflowers from the hedgerows and sometimes peeking into empty bird's nests hidden away amongst the branches of the mixed bushes and shrubs that made up the hedgerows of Kent. Once I found a beautiful, abandoned, perfectly shaped green-blue robin's egg.

One day when I was strolling along the lane, I found pink and white dog roses with beautiful golden stamens growing in the hedgerow. I wanted to pick them, but there were too many thorns. Further along the lane, I spotted some tall purple foxgloves together with sweet-smelling creamy, meadowsweet. (Oh, how I loved that heady scent, and still do.)

I picked some pink and yellow honeysuckle, together with some white moon daisies, scarlet poppies with black smudged centres, pale pink ladies smock, frothy cow parsley, curly bracken and many others. Then with my bounty, I wandered home to the cottage. Once there, I sat on the front step and tied the flowers into bunches with long pieces of grass; I arranged them on the front step pretending it was my flower shop. As I sat down next to the flowers, the warmth of the sun and the smell of new-mown hay filled my senses, and I thought, " This must be what heaven is like."

There was a small stream at the back of the cottage, running through the garden bordered with stinging nettles. One day I stood looking at the stream, listening to the sound of it tumbling over the small rocks as it went. I was wondering what it would be like if I were to fall in.

The next thing I knew, I was in the water. I had somehow slid down the bank through the stinging nettles and into the stream.

Luckily Sheila happened to be home; she was having a cup of tea with Mrs. Watney. Hearing my shout, she ran to my aid and pulled me out of the muddy stream. The nettles had stung my arms and legs, making red wheals that were quite painful. Luckily, my sister found a couple of large dock leaves growing nearby, and as she rubbed them on the stings. The pain magically subsided. I learned to steer clear of nettles after that!

Mrs. Watney minded an empty cottage along the road from hers. It was a pretty little cottage with a red climbing rose growing by the door, encircling it, making an arch. Every morning she took me with her to go and open the windows "to air the rooms." Every evening, we went again to close them. I can remember the wonderful, warm summer feeling in that cottage as the sun streamed into the empty rooms and the scent of the flowers outside filled the air as we threw open the windows. I would so love to have lived there.

I had such a lovely time in the country. It was truly magical with all the wildflowers, insects, birds and animals, and all the different scents.

One time I got to go with my sister, Sheila, to the local brownie troupe. As Sheila was their "Brown Owl," I was allowed to be a brownie for the day. I loved dancing with the other girls around the giant red-spotted toadstool singing,

> *"We're the brownies, here's our aim. Lend a hand*
> *and play the game".*

Then we proceeded to play games and learned to tie knots with lengths of rope. Because I was younger than them, the girls took great care of me, and I wallowed in all the attention I was getting.

When it was time to return home, I was as brown as a berry from roaming the country lanes in the sunshine. Mummy was pleased to at last see some colour in my face. She had called me "white-faced Annie" before I left. Now she said I looked like a gypsy with my olive complexion and my now darkening hair.

It would soon be my birthday. Daddy had been busy while I was away, and he had made me a present. That September birthday, when he handed me the strangely shaped parcel, I opened it to find the beautiful marionette puppet. It was a gypsy with long black hair. He had fashioned her head from papier-mâché, and her carved wooden jointed legs and arms were attached to strings to make her dance. Thelma had made the gypsy dress, it had a long skirt and a pretty white bodice. I loved my gypsy, and would spend hours making her dance.

Daddy was so clever with his hands. When I was younger, he had made me a wooden man with moveable legs. He was made to walk down a hill, also made of wood. I would play for hours with this beautiful toy.

Daddy even made wooden Calendars. He would carve out the shape of a bird, sometimes a chaffinch or a goldfinch or maybe a robin, and paint it in bright colours. He finished it by gluing a calendar to the base. They made lovely presents.

We also had some wonderful pen and ink sketches he had drawn and framed. Years later, we discovered his sketchbook that he had carried with him through the 1914-1918 war when he was in the army. It was filled with sketches of German soldiers and enemy aircraft. I suppose he used his creativity to release the fear of the times.

3

MAY FESTIVITIES AND A NAKED BIRTHDAY CAKE

It was nearly the end of April, and back at Pelham Road Infant's school, we were getting ready for the May Day festivals. Some lucky girl was going to be the May Queen for the day and wear a long dress and a wreath of flowers on her head. We were going to put on a show for our parents, and some of us would be flower fairies. There would be a ceremony for the crowning of the new Queen, and then we would be dancing around the May Pole. There would be a dancing display where twelve girls dressed as flower fairies would dance the 'Waltz of the Hours' before the May Queen.

I badly wanted to be one of the flower fairies, but I wasn't chosen. However, the girl who was to play the bluebell fairy hadn't been to school for a week because she was sick, so my teacher told me I could take her place. Each day I practiced the dance with the other 'fairies' to the 'Waltz of the Hours' by Tchaikovski. I was so excited as I carefully tried on the deep blue crepe-paper dress with tiny gauze wings attached at the back, and the pretty bell-shaped hat. I couldn't wait for the day to arrive.

Thelma told me I looked every inch a fairy as I was so tiny and had a small oval face with a pointed chin. I diligently practiced the steps at home, and eventually thought I would be good enough to join the other flower fairies and dance before our May Queen.

At last, May Day arrived. The day dawned bright and sunny as I skipped happily to school. Mummy was coming to watch me perform, and I felt very special. The May blossom was out on the trees on the school field. I remember there were two kinds, one with dark pink flowers and one with flowers of milky white. The clusters of open flowers with their many orange-tipped stamens gave off a heady, intense perfume. I pushed my nose into the centre of one of the flowers, examining them closely and noticing how pretty they were.

As the new May Queen claimed her flower-decked throne surrounded by her attendants, her long blonde hair blowing in the wind, Mary Small, the new May Queen, was crowned. A wreath of flowers was placed on her head by last year's Queen, then the dancing began.

To my dismay, I discovered that the bluebell fairy had recovered in time for the show. I wistfully watched her dance, knowing that that was the end of my dancing debut. Well, almost, at least I got to dance around the May Pole.

Thinking that I would be performing, I had not practiced dancing around the Maypole. The ribbon I was holding got tangled up with the next girl's ribbon. I was mortified as the design that we were supposed to achieve with the ribbons became a tangled mess. Thankfully, our teacher came to our rescue, pointing the way to go so that it wasn't a complete disaster. Thank goodness!

May also signalled the start of the summer season. We were allowed to move from the playground to the school field as the grass had dried out now. We were now allowed to take balls and skipping ropes to school.

Mummy had bought me a new skipping rope with coloured wooden handles from Woolworth's in the Broadway, but I didn't seem to have enough puff to do much jumping. Instead, I would play with a tennis ball, bouncing it on the ground and against the school wall. As I played, I recited:

"One two three alary
My ball's in the dairy
Don't forget to fetch it Mary
One two three alary."

June came and went, and then as the summer warmed, we were into July. Now we would break up for the summer holidays.

As I had reached the age limit for the infant's school, it was time for my class to move on to the next school in September. So, on the last day of term, we said our goodbyes to the teachers and ran home, looking forward to the six long weeks of school holidays.

Even though school was closed for the summer, we would still walk to school to have our daily milk. All school children were given a third of a pint of milk each day by order of the government. After the war, the children needed building up as so many of us had been on close-to-starvation diets with all the food on ration for most of the six long war years. We also had to have a spoonful of brown sticky Cod Liver Oil and Malt each day as well. We got this from the clinic when we took my baby brother, Christopher, for his weighing.

Throughout the summer holidays, as I walked to school for my milk each day, I would walk to the end of our garden, through the back gate and turn left. I would walk along the back alleyway, following the narrow pathway which led to the school gates, which were standing open. Sometimes stopping on the route, I would peep through the knotholes in the fence to see into other people's gardens.

Once at the school, I would make my way to the school hall and join the other pupils. I picked up the fat one-third of a pint bottle from the crate, and a straw. After removing the cardboard bottle top, I would lick off the cream, push the straw into the wide-necked bottle and drink the silky, creamy liquid. When it was empty, I would deposit the empty bottle back in the crate. With a full tummy, I strolled back along the pathway and home again.

Daddy decided that we should all learn to grow things, and so he gave us each a small plot of earth along the side of the path to plant whatever we liked.

Christopher beside the gardening plots

Each little parcel was marked with a row of tiles to divide it from its neighbour. I loved Daddy's idea and eagerly took the seeds and some bluebell bulbs to plant in my patch. How delighted I was to see them grow and flower. Unhappily for me though, one day I did something to annoy David and so, to pay me back, he picked one of my bluebells. For some reason known only to him, he stuffed it in his ear. Unfortunately, for him, he ended up with earache.

I was eager to be a ballerina. I was fascinated with the art, but there was no chance of Mummy ever being able to afford the lessons. So, I would get books from the library on ballet and practice the steps in my bedroom. Standing on the points of my toes in bare feet made them hurt too much to continue.

One day, as I was practicing, my sister Betty came into my bedroom."Right," she announced, "if you are any good, I will pay for dancing lessons for you."

Now that she was earning, Betty felt that she could afford to do this. I was so excited at the prospect of being able to learn to dance correctly, so I smiled at her, grateful that she would do this for me. Betty settled herself on my bed and smiling, said, "Okay, dance!"

There was no music, and I hadn't a clue what she wanted me to do. Although there were only about three feet by two feet of space beside the bed, I did a few steps and moved my arms around, trying to look graceful.

"No," she said, as she flounced out of the room without a backward glance, "you are not good enough!"

I was so upset and disappointed that I sat on the bed and cried. For now, I would never be a ballerina.

I made friends with the girl who lived across the road from us. She was two years younger than me and lived in one of the first two semi-detached houses that followed on from the terraced ones. Her name was Diana Hobbs, and she lived with her parents and younger twin brothers. Her father had a twin brother too. They were completely identical, so I never quite knew whether I was talking to Diana's father or her Uncle. I also never knew to which of her brothers I was speaking.

Diana and I were always making up dancing steps, and so we decided to have a concert in her garden. We bought some crepe-paper, and I made a half-hoop out of a bendy branch. I decorated it by winding coloured crepe-paper around it and sticking on crepe-paper flower shapes. We decided that Diana had to dance while holding the branch in her hands above her head. We practiced and practiced.

On this particular day, my mother had an old friend, Mrs. Gwilliam, come to visit her at our house. We knew her as Auntie Gwilliam. Wanting to have some quiet chat-time, Mummy told me to go out and play with Diana. While we were playing, Diana invited me into her house. We walked into their front room. There, on a table in the middle of the room, stood a beautiful, large, iced birthday cake. Diana went over to it and picked off a piece of the pink and white icing and ate it. "It's lovely," she said, turning to me, "you try some."

I tried a piece, and before we realized what we were doing, the cake stood there, almost entirely naked of all the icing sugar. We stopped and gazed in shock at the naked cake. At that moment, Diana's mother thinking that we were unusually quiet, entered the room. She took one look at the cake and hit the roof in anger. "What have you done?" She shouted.

We both stood there looking sheepish, unable to think of anything to say. Mrs. Hobbs turned to me, as I backed away from her. "You go right home, and tell your mother what you have done, or I will come and tell her!" She yelled at me, waving her arms.

I ran home, but Auntie Gwilliam was still visiting, so I said nothing. Mrs. Hobbs, who could not contain herself any longer, came over and announced to Mummy and Auntie Gwilliam that Diana and I had ruined the Birthday cake that she had made for the twins. I was mortified! Mrs. Hobbs was going to make sure that I was punished, and paused to see what my Mother would say.

Both Mummy and Auntie Gwilliam looked very crossly at me and asked me why I did it.

"Well, Diana told me to, and it tasted so nice," I replied feebly, staring at the floor, shuffling my feet and feeling decidedly uncomfortable.

Auntie Gwilliam turned her head away. I am sure my mother and her friend were trying hard not to laugh, but they told me to go to my room and stay there, and they would deal with me later! Mollified, Mrs. Hobbs left.

Auntie Gwilliam lived in St. Albans, which is North of London in the County of Hertfordshire. When my parents were first married, they lived in Blakemere Road, Welwyn Garden City. Daddy used to work at the Welgar Shredded Wheat factory there. Mrs. Gwilliam had been a neighbour of theirs until she moved to St. Albans. Since then, she and my mother had kept in touch by letter.

Shortly after Mrs. Gwilliam returned home, Mummy received a letter from her inviting her to go and visit for a weekend. At this time, Sheila had some holiday time owing to her. She realized the need for my mother to have some time away, and so Sheila suggested that she would look after Thelma and Betty, the boys and Daddy. Mummy decided to take me with her, for company. So, now I was to go on my first holiday alone with my Mother.

4

BUBBLES AND CHICKENS

HAPPILY FOR US, SATURDAY DAWNED FAIR. DADDY CARRIED OUR suitcase stopping and changing hands occasionally. He had come to see us off on the bus. I excitedly skipped along with my parents. As we walked up Woolwich Road, I wondered what this new adventure would bring.

We were to catch the bus to Bexleyheath Station from the Clock Tower. I kissed Daddy goodbye, and Mummy gave Daddy a kiss and a hug. He placed our suitcase under the stairwell of the bus while I climbed the steps to the top deck. Mummy followed. We sat in the back seat and waved to Daddy until we couldn't see him anymore.

It was the first time I had been on the top deck of a bus and loved the new view of the world that it afforded me. We didn't usually travel upstairs as it was for people who smoked, and the smoke would make my Mother and I cough.

In the bus, I was level with the tops of the trees. I marvelled at the new outlook, and noticed that the people seemed much smaller from this elevated viewpoint. As the bus rattled along, I soon got tired of looking out of the window, and the rocking of the vehicle began to lull me to sleep. The bus driver was running late, and so to make up his schedule, he put his foot down and then he would break hard at each bus stop or traffic lights. With the erratic movements, my stomach began to churn.

"Mummy, I don't feel very well," I said, holding my stomach. The next thing I knew was that I was sick on the floor. Fortunately, there were no other passengers, so, thank goodness, no one saw me. At the next stop, my mother decided it might be better if we were to ride downstairs, so we slowly and carefully descended the steep stairs, and sat down on the long seat by the entrance.

While Mummy apologized to the conductor for the mess that I had made, he looked at my white face and said kindly, "Don't worry, lady, worse things happen at sea."

Luckily, we only had a few more stops to go before we reached the train station, and we also didn't have too long to wait before the train arrived, puffing to a halt.

Mummy and I climbed into the "Ladies Only" carriage. My mother slid our case in front of her legs. It was too heavy for her to lift into the luggage rack. I was still feeling a little 'green,' and I recalled my last ride on a train, when Thelma, Brian and I returned from our evacuation to Padiham. Back then, we had travelled in a long corridor carriage, whereas the "Ladies Only" carriage was simply a single carriage without a table.

I looked out of the window at the back gardens of the houses we passed. Each one seemed, to me, to look the same as the last, and I chattered to my mother.

When we arrived at our destination, Auntie Gwilliam was waiting to greet us. "Hello!" It's lovely to see you," she said, beaming, and gave us both a hug. Then taking our case, she turned to me. "You look a bit peaky, dear."

"She was sick on the bus." My mother told her.

"Oh dear," she clucked sympathetically, "but never mind, you will soon feel better. We go this way, it's not far." She said, smiling as she led us along the road.

Auntie Gwilliam lived in a bungalow on a hill. The front garden had a long lawn that sloped down to the main road. Auntie and my Mother were looking forward to a 'good old chinwag' and catching up on all the latest news. So, Auntie presented me with a clay bubble pipe and some soapy water to keep me busy. I sat on the grass in the front garden, watching the traffic and blowing bubbles, and the two ladies went back into the house. Auntie couldn't wait to tell Mummy all her news.

I looked around me, there was a lovely feel to this sloping green lawn. I don't know why, but I have loved grassy slopes ever since. I dipped my clay pipe into the soapy mixture and blew bubbles. I watched as the bubbles detached themselves from the bowl of the pipe and floated away on the breeze, the sun catching the rainbows on them as they drifted skywards.

A truck went by, carrying soldiers, and then another, and another. They all cheered and waved at me as I blew my bubbles and Mummy and her friend came out to see what all the noise was. They both laughed when they saw the attention I was attracting, and we all stood and waved together. We were proud of our soldiers who had fought and won the war for us, and we wanted them to know this.

"Well," said Auntie, "after all this excitement, you had better come in and wash your hands, lunch is ready."

Auntie Gwilliam had prepared a salad for us with sliced hard-boiled eggs and slices of ham off the bone. Then, for dessert, there was apple pie and cheese and biscuits. It was delicious, and Mummy said how nice it was to be waited on for a change. I helped my Mother dry the dishes while Auntie washed them, then, as soon as everything was clean and tidy, we decided to go out and see the sights. We had a lovely time. Auntie took us shopping at the outdoor market in the middle of the city, and then we wandered around the shops.

That night Mummy and I slept in the same bed. It was lovely to cuddle up with her, and I slept like a log. We were awoken to the smell of bacon frying, "Ooh, what a lovely smell, it's my favourite," I said, jumping out of bed. After a quick wash, I quickly pulled on a cotton dress, and a pink knitted cardigan, while Mummy brushed my hair. Then, we were ready for breakfast, hurrying down the stairs to find the source of that beautiful aroma.

Auntie was busy in the kitchen tending to the frying pan, and so she got me to watch the toast under the grill so that it didn't burn. When all the bread was brown, we sat down to a lovely cooked breakfast of toast, bacon, tomatoes and eggs with golden yolks, fried until they were brown and crispy around the outside.

"I thought you might like to have a look round St. Albans Abbey today," Auntie remarked, "and then we could perhaps have a picnic in the park."

"Ooh, yes, please!"

It didn't take long to prepare a picnic, and with Auntie carrying the food and Mummy the drink, I brought up the rear with a tartan rug to spread on the grass, rolled up and carried under my arm.

We caught the bus to Verulanium, where the Roman ruins were. Once there, we decided that it made more sense to have the picnic first so that we didn't have to carry the food around for too long. So, we found a cool place under the trees. Sitting on the tartan rug and enjoying the food Auntie had prepared for us was an enjoyable experience. We ate cheese and tomato sandwiches, lovely fruitcake, biscuits and shiny red apples.

Before long, it was time to see the Abbey. It was ancient and magnificent, with high arching ceilings and beautiful stone carvings. As we wandered through the cool building, I was amazed. I had never seen anything quite like this. It was much, much larger and grander than the Congregational Church in Bexleyheath.

We came back out into the brilliant sunshine. We wandered along until we came to the old High Street with its dark beamed, medieval buildings and cobblestone streets. "This looks just like Padiham, where I stayed during the war," I thought. We wandered past the shops again, but all too soon, it was time to catch the train home. I couldn't wait to tell Daddy, Thelma and the boys what a lovely time we had had, and all that we had done and seen.

When we got home, Daddy was so pleased to see us and proudly showed us the box he had been making. It was about two feet long by one foot wide and lightly varnished. The top came off and had a central point for a light bulb, which fitted inside a circular area of the closed box. Some chicken wire replaced one end of the box. He told us that he had decided to get some baby chicks so that we could have lovely fresh eggs. It was a long time since we had kept hens. The last ones ended up as dinner for us during the war, to help stretch out our meagre rations.

We were very excited waiting for Daddy to come home with the chicks. Brian and I sat on the window ledge in the front room, eagerly waiting for him. We soon saw him coming up the road carrying a cardboard box with holes in it.

Brian and I ran to open the door, and we all filed into the kitchen where his wooden box stood proudly on the kitchen dresser. As we all gathered around, Daddy took the top off. He then opened the cardboard box and very gently cupped his large hands around one chick at a time, placing each fluffy yellow chick carefully into their new home.

Daddy turned to Mummy. “They are Rhode Island Reds,” he announced with pride, as he put the cover back and switched on the light. “This will keep them warm until they are big enough to go into our chicken run, at the end of the garden.”

Each day we would peek into the box, listening to the chicks happily cheeping away. We made sure their feed trough was well-filled, and the water container topped up with clean water.

Gradually the chicks started to grow feathers, and Christopher loved to play with them in the garden. He would squat down beside the box. Daddy had also made the little wooden trough for their food, and we took turns to feed them.

Christopher feeding the chicks. Note the cloth hanging from the window. It was hooked across to keep the sun out. Circa 1945

Finally, they were large enough to be moved to the hen run at the end of the garden, and it wasn't long before we were getting lovely brown eggs for our breakfast.

As soon as it was light, each morning, they would begin to cluck. I would take a china bowl and collect the eggs, still warm, and some with bits of straw and mud attached. I would bring them back and, after carefully washing and drying them, I put them in the egg rack in the larder. It was so lovely to see it full of our eggs again. They tasted so much better than the ones we got from Perk's, the grocer's shop up by the Clock Tower. Many-a-time their eggs were bad and smelled terrible when broken, even though they claimed to be "The firm that never sells a bad egg." We knew differently, and we often had to complain about their eggs.

At Easter, Daddy would take the eggs while we were asleep, and with some waterproof crayons, he painted faces on them. Each one was a different character, and there were ladies with black hair, clowns, pirates with a patch over the eye, and many other characters. On Easter Sunday, we took great delight in cracking the tops of their 'heads' as they sat in the eggcups. Mummy would cut our buttered toast into strips that we called "soldiers." We dipped them into the soft golden yolk, yummm! It seemed a shame to destroy his handiwork, but we got a lot of pleasure out of them. We were always surprised with the new characters he would come up with for the following Easters.

I was nearly eight, and Brian and I continued to sleep in the same bedroom. One day he showed me a large suitcase he was keeping under his bed. He pulled it out and clicked open the lid. Inside there was a bottle of Tizer and a bag of cream buns. "We can have a midnight feast tonight," he said excitedly. "I have been saving these!"

I thought that was a great idea, and impatiently waited until it was time to go to bed. We waited until Mummy had come to say our prayers with us,

> *"Thank you for the world so sweet,*
> *Thank you for the food we eat,*
> *Thank you for the birds that sing*
> *Thank you, God, for everything.*
> *Amen*
> *God Bless Daddy, Mummy,*
> *Sheila, Betty, Thelma, Brian, David and*
> *Christopher,*

and make Wendy a good girl.
Amen.

Later I would add, "And God Bless every living creature in the whole world," because I didn't want to leave anything out.

Brian opened the case and handed me a cream bun. I eagerly bit into it. It was hard and stale, and the cream was sour. "Eeoow, how long have you had this?" I asked him. "Oh, only about two weeks," my brother replied airily.

Still trying to get rid of the taste of the sour cream, I asked for a drink of Tizer.

"I have just drunk the last drop," Brian said with a big grin.

So, I hit him, and he hit me back. I yelled, and Mummy's voice from downstairs called, "Go to sleep or I will bang your heads together!" Of course, she had no intention of carrying out her threat, but it made us settle down nonetheless.

5

A NEW SCHOOL

David and Christopher became close, and they would love to wrestle with each other in the hall. Christopher would say, "David, let's play Jack and Bilt." (He meant Bill, but somehow it became Bilt) "I'll be Bilt," he would say and fling himself at David, while David would grab him and hold him to the floor saying, "much pain must be endured."

The summer holidays had come to an end, and so now it was time for me to start attending the Junior School in Church Road. It was where we had boarded the bus to take us to Bexleyheath Station for our evacuation. That seemed a lifetime away now.

On that first day of school, I felt very grown-up. I crossed over Woolwich Road and walked along the path between the two senior school fields, opposite the end of Pelham Road together with Mummy and my two small brothers. She had tucked both Christopher and David into the pushchair.

Mummy had made sure that my hair was tidy. She folded my long plaits in half and tied them with a bow behind each ear. I felt very grown-up and skipped along beside my mother and brothers until we came to the high wall surrounding Christ Church cemetery. Brian had told me that this was where they buried the dead people, but I didn't want to think about that so kept on skipping hurriedly past. We passed the girl's Central School, where my sister Betty had attended.

Finally, we reached Church Road and, kissing my two brothers goodbye, my Mother retied the ribbon bow on one of my doubled-over plaits. My hair had become quite long now and was sometimes a challenge to keep tidy.

Alone now, I walked gingerly through the tall metal gates into the playground, surrounded by a low brick wall, topped with a metal fence. Looking around at the other children, I noticed some standing alone like me, and some stood huddled in deep conversation, letting out the occasional nervous giggle. Others were playing with balls or skipping ropes. I felt somewhat lost and turned and looked for Mummy, but she had left already. She thought it would be easier for me if she didn't hang around. Besides, she wanted to walk back the other way, up the Broadway, and do some shopping while she was out.

I was rather small for my age. Some of the girls were much bigger than me, and I was feeling somewhat intimidated as I looked up at the two-story Victorian school building. It was not unlike the school I went to in Padiham, but it still seemed so huge after the single-storied infant's school I had just left.

A teacher appeared on the steps by the entrance with a handbell, which she rang several times. After lining up, we had to march in a single file into the hall, and then sit down on the floor. As I sat there, I looked around me. The hall was similar to the one at the school I had attended in Padiham, and it bought back the memories of that place.

It had a stage at one end where the teachers were all sitting in a row facing us. The wooden floor was well polished and smelled of beeswax, and the classrooms surrounded the hall. I looked around at the walls, which were tiled halfway up, with shiny brown tiles. Above the tiles were posters of different countries with their names printed beneath. India had pictures of elephants, Africa had a lion. The poster of Holland had tulip fields, and a strange country I hadn't yet heard of, had unusual triangular buildings and camels. I recited the letters to myself, E.G.Y.P.T. and announced what it was: "Eggyput."

I later learned that the word was pronounced 'Ee-jipt.' Well, fancy that!

I had 'butterflies' in my stomach since entering the building. I was feeling somewhat worried, wondering who my new teacher would be. As they called our names, we had to go and stand in line behind the assigned teacher. I felt relief when they finally called my name. My teacher was called Mrs. Sparks, and she looked lovely and smiley, with long hair tied back. She wore a fitted jacket over a wool skirt, silk blouse, and I noticed the shiny buckles on her shoes.

The girl in front of me in the line turned and smiled shyly; I smiled back. She had large brown eyes, short, smooth dark hair with a large white ribbon bow on one side. She wore a pretty striped jumper underneath a brown gymslip. I took an instant liking to her very pretty face. It turned out that she lived on Highland Road, which was beside the police station, off Bexleyheath Broadway, a short walk from the clock tower. "Oh, I know Highland Road," I said, "We go that way to Gravel Hill."

The girl's name was Sylvia Dingley, and we were to become great friends.

Mrs. Sparks clapped her hands sharply to get our attention, and shouted, "Follow me, children." She turned, and we followed in single file through the door, along the corridor and upstairs to our new classroom.

We each had separate wooden desks with lift-up lids and inkwells. There was a pile of exercise books on the teacher's desk, and she picked a girl to hand one out to each pupil.

The girl's name was Mavis Blackmore. She had straight black hair with a ribbon bow on both sides, to keep it off her face. She was also to be the ink monitor. Mavis's job was to keep all the inkwells filled up. The desks had a sloping top with the inkwell sunk into the right-hand corner. An indented ridge ran the width of the desk just below the inkwell, where we kept our wooden pen with the metal nib. Our teacher told us that, at first, we would start with pencils until we had mastered 'joined-up' (cursive) writing. Imagine that, me, doing grown-up writing!

The desks were in four blocks of ten. Sylvia and I sat beside each other, halfway back. I looked around at our new classroom. The large windows looked out onto the playground, the entrance gate, and rows of terraced houses. There was no school field that I could see. But later, when we had a break time, I found it on the other side of the building, surrounded by a high wall. It didn't take me long to get used to my surroundings at the new school. I made many new friends there.

Church Road Junior School. BACK ROW: Wendy, fourth from the left. Dawn Loft, fourth from the right, Mavis Blackmore, far right. Sylvia Dingley is sitting to the left of Mrs. Sparkes. On the floor from left to right is Joyce Heron and Rosina Brett. Marjorie Button is in the row behind them second from the left.

We each had to pay one shilling and eightpence a week for our school dinners, which were served to us in the canteen in the nearby senior Central School. Mummy would put the coins in the corner of an envelope and fold it up into a small package that would fit into my pocket. So, each day, rain or shine, we formed a 'crocodile' and crossed the road outside the school gate. Together, we walked around the corner and up the hill for our midday dinner. Some days it was quite an effort for me to walk up the slope of Belvedere Road, and I would be puffing and blowing by the time we reached the canteen, feeling that all-too-familiar tightness in my chest.

One winter, the insides of my knees were very sore and itchy with eczema. I had scratched them and made them bleed onto my long white socks. I can remember the girl behind me in the crocodile asking me, "Why have you got jam on your legs?"

Inside the canteen were long tables with wooden benches. We would line up for our dinner. The dinner ladies placed the unappetizing meat, cabbage and potatoes, or Swede if there were no potatoes (how I hated Swedes) on our plates. On one occasion, I remember being given whale meat, but I don't think it was very popular. Sometimes we had tapioca for pudding. It had currants in it, so we nicknamed it 'tadpoles in paste.'

At dinner, we sat at long tables on long wooden forms (benches), while a teacher would walk around, telling us to "Sit up! And don't slouch."

I really hated ginger pudding and custard, but we had to eat everything on our plates because wasting food would not be tolerated. One day I was left sitting by myself with a plate of ginger pudding in front of me while everyone else had left. The teacher was sitting beside me, trying to make me eat it. I took a mouthful and began to retch. It worried the teacher at the thought of having to clean up my vomit, so she quickly removed the rest and told me to leave. "Oh, thank goodness!" I thought, and ran to find my friends.

My friend Sylvia, together with Rosina Brett, Joyce Heron and Dawn Loft were hovering by the canteen door waiting for me. We linked arms and made our way back down the hill to our school playground, skipping along.

"Did she make you eat it?" Sylvia asked breathlessly. I stopped skipping and unlinked my arms. "No," I replied, looking at her, "I let her think that it was going to make me sick, and she didn't want to have to clear it up!" We all laughed, heartily.

When we got back to school, we had barely enough time to remove our coats and get to the classroom before the bell went for the start of afternoon classes.

That afternoon we were doing English composition and spelling. We were asked to write a sentence showing the meaning of the word 'huge.' I wrote, "The huge, great bulk of the elephant fell on a passing ant." That got me an A-minus.

Then, we were given twenty words to learn how to spell before the following week. We had to copy them from the blackboard into our exercise books. I was an avid reader and never had to study any of these words as spelling came naturally to me.

During the next lesson, which was handicrafts, the teacher was going to teach us how to knit. Happily, I knew how to do that as well. The Aunts in Padiham had taught me how to knit during the war.

Mrs. Sparks had a box beside her desk. It was filled with balls of wool. Whoever came top of the spelling test was allowed to be the first to choose two colours of yarn. I won, and chose the brightest colours I could find. We were going to make mittens and learn how to do the Slip stitch. I couldn't wait to begin. I knitted my mittens in lime green and bright, shocking pink. I thought the colours were lovely together.

We did the slipstitch on the mittens by slipping one stitch in four from the row below. As I watched the pattern evolve, I was very proud of myself. Unfortunately, if we wanted to keep the mittens, we had to pay for them. I never got to take them home, or to wear them when I had finished, as Mummy couldn't afford it.

One day we had two new pupils join our class. They were German Jews. We had no idea or understanding of what the Jews had suffered in Germany during the war. I don't think many of us knew what a Jew was, or we might have been kinder to these poor girls. Our concern was that they were German. We had been taught to hate all Germans because of the bombing of our country, and so, sadly, we teased them unmercifully. This continued until the poor girls could take no more of our unkind taunts, and left the school, never to return.

We were taught not to trust, and to fear everything German, so we were relieved that they had gone. I felt uneasy when they were there. None of us could understand what these girls said when they spoke, and I don't think they could understand us either. Looking back, I think the teachers could have done more to help us to understand, but maybe they felt the same as us about the Germans. There was still much that we all needed to learn.

Things were still scarce in England, and it was difficult to get school writing books. Our teacher, therefore, was delighted when a consignment of exercise books arrived from Canada, together with some food parcels.

The books were called 'jumbo exercise books' and were huge. They had a picture of an elephant on the cover and contained unlined rough paper. I can remember how, when writing in these books, my writing got bigger and bigger and more slanting by the time it reached the bottom of the page. I found it so hard to write in a straight line, without any guiding lines.

School finished at 4 o'clock now instead of 3:30 pm, which was the time the infant's school finished. After school, we would cross the road and go to the little shop on the corner. If we had any money, we would buy sweets; my favourite was sherbet powder in a little bag with a licorice straw to suck it through. Often the sherbet would go down the wrong way, and I would end up coughing, but I loved the way it melted in my mouth, even though it made my tongue bright yellow and sore. I also enjoyed the sherbet lemons; they were lemon-shaped boiled sweets with sherbet in the center. My next favourite was a penny Oxo cube, which I would nibble away at, all the way home. It reminded me of Marmite, and I loved Marmite, the meat extract that Mummy would put in our sandwiches.

Mrs. Sparks was an accomplished violinist, and during singing lessons, she would play the violin. One day, we were each allowed to have a go. As I was tiny, the violin seemed as big as me. I tucked the polished wooden instrument under my pointed chin. Passing the bow across the strings, I produced a sound that would have sent all the cats, for miles around, scurrying to hide. My friend Sylvia stuffed her fingers in her ears and wore a pained expression. Both my teacher and I concluded that the violin wasn't for me!

That Christmas, we were to put on a school concert featuring people from other nations. I was to be a Chinese boy, and Sylvia, a Chinese girl. On the day of the show, we changed into our Chinese costumes and coolie hats. The teacher decided that we should look a little more Chinese, so she brought some Coleman's mustard powder. After first spreading our faces with cold cream, she proceeded to spread the mustard over the top, to give us a yellow tinge. However, by the end of our performance, we were both in tears as the mustard had burned our skin.

We washed off the offending mustard and got a profuse apology from the teacher who told us she “had no idea this would happen.” We went home with bright red faces, and a lesson learned!

6

A TRIP TO THE SEASIDE

It was the summer of 1948, and Daddy looked up as the news came on the radio. "Well, it's about time."

A big smile lit up Arthur's face as he listened to an announcement that we would now have a National Health Service. Now all visits to the doctor and all medicines would be free! That would make such a difference to him; with all the medications we needed, Daddy's wages didn't go far. Now he would be able to worry less. At last, things were looking up!

That same week, Mummy got a letter from Auntie Gwilliam. While we had been visiting her, she had told us about the holiday bungalow she owned at Camber Sands near Rye in Kent. Auntie had indicated to Mummy that we could all spend a free holiday there if we wished. Mummy read the letter and smiled, "How lovely! Auntie says the bungalow is free the last two weeks of August. We can go and have a holiday there!" she said with a smile.

Mummy wrote back to Auntie then and there, accepting her kind offer, and Auntie replied with the directions of how to get to the bungalow, so now it was arranged. We were all so excited; it would be our very first holiday together. Two whole weeks by the seaside, hooray!

We were to get the Green Line bus, pick up another coach to take us to Rye and finally a taxi to the bungalow situated almost on the beach at Camber Sands. So, our parents, Thelma, Brian, David, and myself, bags and cases, and with Christopher in the pushchair, set out for the bus station. It was at the top end of Pelham Road, round the corner and on the other side of Erith Road.

After our first bus journey, we decided we would stop at a café opposite the station for a drink and a bite to eat. A bored, skinny waitress in a floral apron, and with hair pulled back under her cap, was leaning on the counter, smoking. She looked over at us as we entered and, without a word, disappeared through a door to the back kitchen.

"Well, she was helpful," Daddy remarked under his breath, and with Brian's help, pushed two tables together so that we could all sit down.

Christopher was now learning to drink out of a cup without spilling the drink. So, when the waitress reappeared, Daddy ordered a plate of biscuits, five glasses of lemonade for us, and tea for him and Mummy.

My mother took Christopher out of the pushchair and placed him on her knee, offering him a glass of lemonade. Christopher took a bite out of the glass!

Mummy was horrified and, retrieving the glass from his mouth, she checked to make sure his mouth was not bleeding. The waitress, annoyed, bought her another glass, and Christopher did the same thing again! After that, the waitress bought a thick china cup and finally, Christopher got to drink without mishap.

When we had finished eating, Mummy gathered us all together, while Daddy paid the waitress. This had taken longer than we had anticipated it would, so we had to hurry if we were to catch the next bus before it went without us.

We did catch the bus in time. As we all scrambled aboard the Green Line coach, the driver helped Daddy place the cases in the luggage locker. I sat next to Thelma and Brian and with David on Daddy's lap and Christopher on Mummy's, the bus set off! We were all so excited. Thelma, Brian and I chatted for the entire journey.

I was so looking forward to seeing the sea for the second time in my young life. (The first time being when Auntie Dora and Auntie Adelia took Thelma and me to visit Morecambe during the war.)

The coach rattled along winding green country lanes with high hedges either side. Sometimes we got to see over the top of the hedge, and I happily gazed at the cows and sheep grazing in the lush fields. Gradually the scenery changed and became less hilly and with fewer trees. It was marshland here, and tall rushes grew up out of the soggy ground. We were going through Romney Marshes, and there were sheep everywhere happily grazing, how we loved the lambs with their long tails.

We finally arrived at the old town of Rye, with its medieval-looking buildings and cobbled streets. The bus stopped, and as we alighted, we spotted a row of taxis. Daddy raised his hand to attract the elderly taxi driver, who then helped us put our luggage in the boot, and then we were off again.

The taxi rattled along the old-fashioned cobble-stoned streets, shaking us up and down, until eventually, the road became smooth as we left the town far behind. We were on our way to the sea! Hooray!

The sun had disappeared behind a large cloud, but Brian and I didn't care, our excitement rose as we spied the sea in the distance. It still seemed a long way off, but before long, we found that we were almost at the beach.

The winding sand-strewn road led us to Auntie Gwilliam's bungalow. Tufts of grass grew from the enormous sand dunes that were in front of it, obstructing the view of the sea. The taxi stopped in front of a small square house, surrounded by a fence and a small gate. We were here at last! Hooray!

Mummy opened the gate and walked up the short, sandy path. Daddy found the key, which had been left under a bucket by the door. He opened the door, picked up the cases, and we all spilled into the hall.

We went through to the kitchen. Mummy started unpacking the food and filling the larder. I was intrigued to see that there was no tap in the kitchen sink, but instead, there was a pump. This would be used to pump the water.

We explored the three bedrooms, deciding who would sleep where. Once we had decided, we unpacked our clothes. As we didn't have many, it didn't take long. Then Brian and I decided we would go and explore.

"Don't go too far," Mummy called after us anxiously. "We'll have something to eat just as soon as I have sorted myself out."

The sun had appeared again as now small puffy clouds raced across the sky. Going through the gate of the bungalow, Brian and I found ourselves on the dunes.

As the strong wind whipped up the sand, it stung our legs, but it was lovely and soft to walk on, so I took off my sandals, which were now full of sand anyway. I stepped carefully, trying to avoid the rolls of barbed wire strewn randomly on the beach. The barbed wire was leftover from the war and was used to hinder any landing enemy (or innocent child).

Once we were clear of the wire, we ran down to the water's edge. It was a beautiful afternoon, and the waves lapped gently at the shoreline. I gazed out to sea, watching the sunbeams sparkling on the water. I tucked my dress into my knickers, and began to paddle at the edge of the water. Brian removed his sandals and paddled along beside me.

Memories of Morecambe came flooding back, but there was no town here, just miles and miles of soft sand and dunes. It was so lovely to sniff the salty air and feel the sun on my legs and arms. The wind tugged at my hair, blowing it across my face. Seagulls whirled and dived and swooped into the sea, calling to each other.

Then we came across a large, grey, concrete building with slits for windows. It had a padlocked door.

"It's a gun turret!" Brian exclaimed, "They could machine gun the enemy from here, brrrrrr," he said, holding an imaginary machine gun.

We gazed with interest at the ugly monstrosity. It gave me a horrid feeling as I pictured what Brian had told me, and I began to think about the bombs and the war again.

After a while, realizing that he was hungry, Brian said, "We had better be getting back now."

We had wandered along the beach and had walked further than we realized. As Brian and I made our way back over the dunes back towards the bungalow, we discovered that we had lost our bearings. We approached a large building, and could see that it housed an amusement arcade. Enthralled, we went in and wandered around, mouths open.

The flashing lights and loud music were all new to us. We had no money with us, so we were unable to play on the slot machines. I watched as other children put their pennies into the machines and I wished that I had some money, so that I could have a go. Then I had a brainwave - "Let's go and tell Mummy," I suggested, "she might give us some pennies to put in the machines."

We did, eventually, find our way back to the bungalow. When we got there, we found our parents struggling to get some water from the rather old pump in the kitchen. Without a tap and only the arm of the pump, we had to push the arm up and down to get any water. Mummy was not enthralled with this, as it took some strength to do, which was something she did not have much of. She leaned on the side of the stone sink for a moment, to catch her breath.

"Where have you been," she asked us crossly, as she struggled to breathe. She had been worrying that we might be lost. "We found some games in a big building," I replied. Daddy looked up. "What do you mean?" he asked.

We told him about how we had come across the amusement arcade on our way home. "You must come and see it," I told him, urgently, grabbing his hand. "Just wait until we get this pump working," he replied, "Your mother wants to wash the dishes before we use them." Finally, the water began to flow. So, leaving Mummy to the dishes, Daddy followed us out to the beach.

We found the arcade again, and as we showed Daddy around, he put his hand in his trouser pocket and gave us each a penny. Unfortunately for me, my penny was lost straight away. Brian decided to try a slot machine with a crane inside. The crane made a squeaky noise and moved across jerkily, hovering over the prizes. Then it dropped down, and the claws closed over a yellow plastic eggcup, raised it and dropped it into a hole. Brian gave a whoop of excitement and, retrieving the eggcup, he held it aloft.

"Look what I won," he yelled with glee. "I'm going to have a boiled egg for my breakfast in this!"

Daddy gave us each one more penny, they were consumed in a flash, and then he decided we had had enough for one day. After rounding us up, we all made our way back.

At the cottage, Mummy was busy slicing bread in the kitchen. She had taken an Ephedrine pill, and her difficult breathing had eased. She was now humming to herself as she spread the bread with a thin film of margarine. After sprinkling each slice with sugar, she put the bread on a large plate and carried it to the table in the dining room.

Brian proudly showed her his eggcup. Mummy smiled, "You can get me some more of those. Now go and wash the sand off your hands, both of you."

She had left some water in the sink for hand washing, which was just as well as neither Brian, nor I could summon enough strength to work the pump, though we both tried to do it.

The next day, our mother got up early and made some marmite sandwiches for us to take to the beach. We spent all day on the beach. I couldn't remember when we had all done something together like this, and it made such a lovely change.

Before we left, we had told the Mephams, our next-door neighbours from Pelham Road, where we were going, and they came down for a visit, bringing their four-year-old granddaughter, Sandra, with them. Again, we all went to the beach and made sandcastles.

I had quickly discovered that you didn't make castles from the dry sand, but that once it was wet, you could form it into any shape. So I made a sand motorboat for Christopher and Sandra. They spent ages sitting on it.

Wendy and David kneeling, Christopher and Sandra on the sand motorboat

The following days found Brian and I racing to the arcade and winning lots of eggcups, so many, that Mummy was sick of the sight of them by the time we left.

It was a lovely holiday. Thelma, Brian and I spent a lot of time jumping off the highest dunes we could find, I felt fearless, as some of them were quite high, but I realized that with the soft sand to catch me, I could do it.

We also went paddling in the sea and collected shells. My favourite ones were the pink ones like tiny fingernails.

One day we took the bus into the town of Rye, where the streets were narrow and cobbled. The buildings were ancient. Many were timber-framed.

Mummy discovered a sweet shop selling handmade sweets. The window was a curved bay and had bottle glass in it. Looking through the window, I saw rows and rows of jars full of delicious sweets. There were golden twists of barley sugar, black and white cushion-shaped bullseyes, bright yellow sherbet lemons, and chewy brown toffee. There was also delicious fudge, and long sticks of luminous pink rock with 'Rye' printed right through the middle. "I've seen that before," I said, "It was just like the Morecambe rock we had in Padiham," I told Daddy.

There were also various coloured jelly babies and long sticks of licorice. My favourite was the dolly mixtures – a mix of tiny jellies and sandwiches of different coloured confection. They were ideal for playing tea parties with my dolls as they fitted my little doll's plates. It was so hard to choose what to buy and so great not to have the restrictions on them that we had while they were on ration. Now that the war was over, we could purchase as many as we liked. Mummy bought some rock and some dolly mixtures and a few black sticks of licorice.

Mummy and I noticed a wool shop. In the window was a china doll dressed in a red and white striped knitted outfit. I thought it was so beautiful. Mummy said to me, "Stay here and watch Christopher and David," as she and Thelma entered the shop.

I held the handle of the pushchair playing 'peep-bo' with Christopher. After a long while, Mummy emerged from the shop, carrying a bag. I was half hoping she would have the doll with her, but she didn't, it still sat in the window. I took a last longing look at it . Mummy gave us some liquorice to chew on while waiting for the bus to take us back to Camber Sands and the bungalow. We enjoyed the rest of our family holiday together and then it was time to return home. Once we had returned to Bexleyheath, we got back into our routines. Our holiday quickly became a happy memory.

The first week of September always heralded 'back to school' time, and the days were growing shorter now. It was term time again, and time for me to return to Church Road School. David was now six years old and would be starting back at the infants' school that I had left.

There was a chill in the air, and soft white mists drifted across the fields as we made our way to school in the morning. The hedges hung with cobwebs, strung with tiny jewels of water. "Season of mists and mellow fruitfulness…"

I loved this time of the year and the feeling of expectation that hung in the air – because September was my Birthday month!

One day when I was in the bathroom, I noticed a cardboard box under the bath. I quickly finished what I was doing and went to investigate. I got down on my knees on the cold, hard linoleum, and slid the box out from underneath the bath. I took off the lid, and there was a beautiful china doll like the one I had seen in the window of the wool shop. She was dressed in only a pair of knitted knickers. I took her out of the box and cradled her; she had painted brown curly hair and a smiling face.

"It must be a surprise for me," I thought. After all, Thelma is too old for dolls, and my birthday will soon be here, I reasoned. Then, carefully replacing the doll inside her box, I slid it back under the bath. I closed the bathroom door behind me with a secret smile and said nothing to anyone about it.

In the days and weeks that followed, I would visit the doll and take her out of the box. Each time I visited her, she was wearing a new piece of clothing. Until finally, I held her, resplendent in a red and white skirt, jumper and bonnet, also knitted bootees. She was now identical to the doll I had admired in the shop window, back in the town of Rye.

Saturday, the day of my 10th Birthday, arrived. I was presented with the box, which I was now so familiar with. It was wrapped in pretty pink paper, and as I tore it off, I tried to look surprised. However, I didn't fool Sheila. "You knew about her, didn't you?" she accused me.

I went red and nodded. Sheila had noticed how the box appeared to move to different positions under the bath. I had not been smart enough to always put it back in the same place. "Oh, but I love her," I cried. They all laughed.

Mummy had bought the wool and pattern when she went into that shop in Rye and had knitted the doll's clothes each evening while I was in bed.

"Oh, well," Sheila, said smiling, "We have another surprise for you." I took my eyes off the doll for a moment to look at her. "Thelma, Betty and I have clubbed together. We are going to buy you a new dress." She announced.

I jumped up and down. I couldn't remember ever having had a new dress before. All my clothes, and most of my shoes were hand-me-downs from my three sisters.

So, Sheila, Betty, Thelma and I set out for Hides, the department store near the clock tower. As we walked up Woolwich Road, we met Mrs. Vevers. She had moved into our old house in Woolwich Road.

"Well, hello, Woosey," she said to me and then turning to my sisters, "You look like the three graces."

My sisters smiled and passed the time of day and then we continued. "I wish she wouldn't call me that," I said, frowning. "It's because she likes you," Betty said with a grin. "Well, I don't like it," but by then, my mind turned to the matter in hand, my new dress!

In the children's department, I gazed around at all the lovely clothes. My eyes settled on a pale blue taffeta dress with short puffy sleeves and a gathered skirt that tied at the back with a sash that made a huge bow. It was love at first sight, and I could hardly contain myself as I tried it on. There never were clothes like this in the Red Cross second-hand shop just along the road.

My sisters stepped back. They all agreed that it was the one for me. So after having the dress wrapped in tissue and put in a box, I proudly carried it to the ribbon haberdashery department. Sheila chose and purchased a yard of pale blue ribbon to match the dress. "For your hair," she announced.

I was so happy, that I skipped nearly all the way home. Once there, I couldn't wait to show Mummy. "Well, go and try it on!" she urged. The dress was such a pretty blue, and so soft I thought, as I lovingly stroked the shiny taffeta. Then, quickly climbing out of my old clothing, I put it on. Sheila found the new ribbon and combed out my plaits so that she could fix it to my hair. Then, after tying a bow, she stepped back to survey how I looked. "Get the camera Mummy, let's take a picture," she said.

Thelma, Sheila, Betty and Wendy (wearing her new birthday dress. Circa 1945

My mother told us to go into the garden while she found Daddy's box camera. She would take a picture of her four girls together. Afterwards, Mummy smiled at me and said, "You look beautiful, but, always remember, if you want to be beautiful, you must think beautiful thoughts."

I smiled back at her as I took in what she was saying to me. With so many brothers and sisters, it wasn't often that I received so much attention from her, and I liked the way it made me feel.

It was a lovely birthday and to finish it off; we had a Birthday tea with blancmange and jelly. Mummy had made me a Birthday cake with ten candles on. As I blew them out, I made a wish, and everyone sang Happy Birthday.

Oh, it was!

7

FAIRS AND FERRY BOATS

OUR LIVES WERE CHANGING NOW. IT SEEMED THAT NOW, AT LAST, it was true, we could, indeed, begin to live our lives without the dreaded air raid siren stopping what we were doing every minute of the day and night.

One evening I was in bed, and had just fallen asleep when I felt Betty shaking me. I sat up quickly, mistakenly thinking it was another trip to the shelter, and rubbed my eyes sleepily.

"Come on," she said, pulling me out of bed. "We are going to the fair!"

As I scrambled out of bed, Betty helped me to get dressed. A fair had come to Danson Park. Having heard about it, Daddy thought that it was "about time we had some fun." So, he had planned for us to all go and enjoy ourselves after tea that evening. The day seemed very long but soon we were hurrying along the road. Arthur, Doris and their seven children caught the bus to Welling at eight-thirty. The bus took us to the Crook Log Public house, which was the nearest stop to the park. We alighted the bus and crossed the road to enter the fair by the tall iron park gates. Then, we followed the long driveway and the crowds of people who were also determined to enjoy themselves. Before long, we found ourselves amid the bright lights, noise and excitement of the shouting stallholders, candyfloss, and hot dog smells of the fair.

How amazing, that we could now have bright lights on anywhere at night without the likelihood of enemy planes seeing us, and dropping their bombs. I wondered how long it would be before I would forget about them altogether.

Daddy bought us some pink candyfloss on a stick. I watched, mesmerized as the man poured the dark pink sugar into the spinning machine, where it was whisked into a soft pink floss. Then he twirled a stick around in the floss until a considerable amount of the froth of spun sugar attached itself to it. He handed it to me, and I bit into the sweet gooey cottonwool-like mass. With the sugar around my mouth, I shared it with my brothers, and we all became very sticky in the process. Christopher grabbed a piece and tried to stuff it into his mouth with a big grin on his face. I think he had more around his mouth than in it, and he sat licking his lips as he tried to retrieve what was left. I wanted to give him the stick, but Mummy stopped me. "Don't give that to him, he will get splinters, or worse," she told me, concerned for her little one's welfare. So I threw it into a wire rubbish basket as we continued strolling around the fairground.

My eyes must have been as big as golf balls. It was the first time I had ever seen a fair. Brian and I shared a car on the bumper cars, or dodgems, but I didn't like it when he crashed into another vehicle. I held tightly onto the sides of the car. Then Thelma, Betty and I rode on the much calmer carousel! It was colourful, and I liked the cheerful music and the beautifully carved brightly painted wooden horses with their flowing manes and flared nostrils. It was a lovely feeling riding those horses and going up and down with them. Holding tightly to the golden barley sugar shaped pole, I turned to Thelma and Betty, riding behind me. I waved, and they grinned and waved back.

After that, we went on the swing boats together. I loved the way you pulled on the long ropes with the red and black fluffy ends to swing yourself into the air. I was a little nervous about how high I was going, but I soon became used to it and started to enjoy myself.

Then we went on the ghost train. I didn't see much because the shrieking and all the strange noises scared me, so I went around with my eyes shut.

We had a go on rolling our pennies down the shoot. At the bottom of the shoot were painted squares with numbers in them. Whatever square it landed on, you could win that number of pennies, but if it fell on one of the lines, the man swept it away. Of course, whichever way you pointed the slide, there wasn't much chance of a rolling penny landing right inside the square, so he was on to a good thing.

We stayed at the fair until the fairground started to close. What a fantastic time we all had. Then, feeling tired but happy, Daddy carried David on his shoulders, and we slowly and reluctantly made our way home. After a mug of cocoa, we were, once more, tucked up in bed and immediately fell asleep.

A year had gone by, and by the time I was eleven, we had a new school teacher, Miss Hutchings. She was a wonderful storyteller and would smile a lot. She had shiny brown hair and would sit on the front of her desk and read aloud to us. The whole class adored her. Through her stories, we were able to escape to the magical places in the tales she read.

I learned a lot in her class. Miss Hutchings was a Canadian, and she had decided that we were to learn and remember at least one new thing each day. One particular day she decided that, before she would let them go home, someone from each of the four rows of desks had to tell her something new that they had learned that day. A girl from each of the first three rows shared something they had learned, but in my row, no one could think of anything. Then, I had a brainwave and put my hand up. "Yes, Wendy, what have you learned today?" she asked.

"I learned that Queen Elizabeth 1st. was the daughter of King Henry 8th," I announced proudly. Miss Hutchings looked baffled. "When did you learn that? You didn't have History today."

"Oh," I replied, feeling very smart, "I think I heard it on the radio this morning Miss." That wasn't true, but the teacher laughed and said we could all go home. I felt very proud of myself as the other girls gathered around and thanked me for getting them out of a fix. After this, Miss Hutchings abandoned the idea of keeping us late – unless, of course, we had misbehaved or arrived late for school.

It was now time for the 'eleven-plus' exams. Those who passed would be going on to Erith Grammar School; those who failed would continue their education at the Central School, which was where we went each day for our school dinner. I didn't want to go to the Grammar School, as it would mean having to catch a bus to Erith, which to me, seemed very daunting. So I was pleased and relieved when I heard that I hadn't passed the exam. It was not surprising, as I had fallen into the habit of gazing into space and daydreaming. I didn't think I could get used to spending a whole day in class without it being punctuated by trips to the air-raid shelter! Many times, when we came to the end of a lesson, I realized that I had not heard a word that the teacher had said.

There were only a few pupils deemed smart enough to go to Erith Grammar, which wasn't surprising considering how our education, up until now, had been so disrupted. My three sisters had gone to the Central School, and now I was following them. Although Sheila and Thelma went on to Bexley County Technical School when they were thirteen, Betty had stayed on at the Central School.

Now I would have to wear a uniform to school. One Saturday, Mummy decided to take me out, together with Thelma, to buy my new school uniform. We walked up to the clock tower in the Broadway and caught a trolley bus, the 696 to Woolwich. We were going to Cuffs, the large department store in the high street. The shop assistants all wore dark dresses with white collars and cuffs and referred to Mummy as "Modem."

We rode on the escalator, taking great care to jump off at the end, just in case our feet got stuck. We found the children's wear department. There was row upon row of school gymslips in varying colours, navy, green, maroon, and the colour I needed, brown. Mummy held different gymslips up against me, and before long, a saleswoman approached us.

"How can I help, Modem," enquired the rather skinny woman with a sniff. She wore her hair in a tight bun and had small glasses on the end of her nose. She reminded me of Olive Oil, the girlfriend of Popeye, the Sailor Man. My mother smiled, feeling a little intimidated.

"I would like a brown gymslip for my daughter," she replied, trying to sound more confident than she was feeling. "She needs a size age 9," she added. (I was quite small for my age.)

The woman looked down her nose at Mummy through the tiny lenses of her glasses, making Mummy feel inferior. However, the assistant found the suitable size gymslip and Mummy held it up against me.

"Would Modem like her to try it on?" she asked, attempting a smile in anticipation of making a sale.

We all walked to the changing room. In the tiny cubicle, I tried on the garment. I gazed at my reflection in the mirror of the cubicle. I seemed taller. The neat box pleats were held together at the waist with a long braided belt, which I had knotted. "Don't tie it too tightly," my mother said, "you don't want to look like a sack of potatoes," she added. We found that it left room for me to grow; it was almost to my ankles. I didn't like the brown colour, but that was the uniform colour, so there was no choice. So, Mummy purchased it.

My mother handed the woman some paper money and coins. She placed them in a pneumatic metal tube, which then went hurtling up and across the ceiling, to the cash office, with a thump. Soon the change and receipt came rushing back with another thud, landing behind the counter. I was fascinated as I watched the network of tubes going back and forth across the store.

With that purchase made, I now needed some new blouses. We chose two lovely crisp white poplin blouses (one to wash and one to wear) and together with two new pairs of white ankle socks, I was all set with my new school uniform. I didn't have to get a blazer as Mummy had kept Thelma's old brown blazer with braid around the collar and a gold and black badge on the pocket. I would be able to wear that with my gymslip.

Thinking back, I don't know how my Mother could afford these clothes for me. She must have had to go without something, but I suppose this was something that she was used to doing. In any case, I never heard her complain about it.

We wandered around the store, marvelling at the beautiful things they had to offer. After descending to the lower ground floor, using the lift this time, we visited their bargain basement. After looking at the prices of these so-called bargains, Mummy remarked ruefully, "Only the rich could afford their bargains." We decided to leave Cuffs for the bustling streets of Woolwich because Mummy had an idea.

"How would you like to go for a ride on the Woolwich Ferry?" She asked us. "Ooh, yes, please!" Thelma and I answered in unison.

So, we made our way towards the Thames River. We had the choice of either going by boat or walking through the tunnel under the water. Both sides of the entrance to the tunnel bore large bullet holes where German planes had strafed the walls during the war. We chose the boat.

The loud screechy cry of seagulls sounded, as two huge birds swooped down, snatching up a morsel of food from the litter carelessly dropped, and then soared again. Two small children were playing alone in the mud at the river's edge. They were filthy, screaming and laughing as they ran through the grey-brown sticky mess.

As we approached the dock, the enormous boat towered over us, waiting to take on the passengers. We walked up the wooden gangway, made our way over to the railing and peered over the side. The water was murky, oily and dirty. Soon, the dense water began to swirl and churn as the boat's engines burst into life. There was a horrible smell of oil as we started to move away from the jetty. It made me feel sick, and I shivered as I was feeling the chill from the wind. Mummy put her arm around me, pulling me towards her and warming me with her body. I looked up and smiled gratefully, happy to have her near me.

I gazed into the grey depths of the water and all the bits of driftwood and debris. Noticing the large patches of oil floating on the surface, making rainbow patterns, I remembered the vivid description of the child who fell into the Canal when we were evacuated. I shivered a second time and grabbed my mother's rough, work-worn hand for comfort.

She turned and pointed to a large square building standing near the water's edge, looking very much like an upturned table with four chimney pot 'legs' sticking up into the air. "That's the Woolwich Power Station," she told us. The enormous brown 'legs' were belching out smoke and polluting the air, looking every bit like four giant cigarettes.

As the ferryboat made its way across the river, sounding its foghorn, a small craft sailed by. The sound made me jump, and Thelma laughed, calling me a "Scaredy Cat."

Thelma turned and ran along the deck, with me running after her. I chased her until our mother called us to stop or else we would get lost or fall overboard. The boat was approaching the land on the other side of the river, so we both ran back to Mummy. Puffing again, we made our way slowly off the boat onto dry land. I felt as though I was still on the boat because my body still seemed to be rocking with the movement of the waves. Slowly I became accustomed to not rocking back and forth. It had been a strange new feeling.

After looking around at the scruffy area of pubs and bombed sites, it didn't take us very long to realize that it was much more attractive on the Southside of the river. So, we decided to return. Mummy had thought that it might be fun to walk back through the tunnel, but because of my asthma attack, we chose instead, to get back on the ferry so that I could breathe the 'fresh' air.

Luckily, we were able to board the same boat as it was moored and waiting for the return passengers. We decided to go below deck this time, as a chill wind was blowing. The strong smell of the engine again made me feel sick, so by the time we arrived on the south side of the river, not only was I puffing, but I also looked a little green. Mummy was beginning to regret her idea of a trip on the ferry.

To add to our woes, we approached the bus station only to see the back of our bus as it left. "Oh, blow!" She exclaimed.

Mummy was getting tired of carrying the shopping. She was also starting to wheeze herself, but as she was so used to feeling like this, for our sakes, she tried to ignore it and plonked herself down on a bench.

Thelma and I sat down either side of her. Placing the bags on the ground between her feet, Mummy put an arm around each of us. I was feeling drained and closed my eyes, my head against her chest. I must have nodded off as I awoke with Thelma tugging at my arm. "Come on, Wendy," she begged, "it's our bus!"

We had an uneventful trip home. With renewed energy, I ran up the garden path and banged on the door knocker. I was dying to try on my new uniform so that I could show it to Daddy. As Brian opened the front door, I rushed past him to find Daddy and tell him all about our trip and show him my new clothes.

Brian told me how Daddy had taken him shopping to the leather shop to get some more shoe leather. This time, it was for Brian's and my shoes.

"...and Mr. Jenner gave me two bullseyes," Brian said with a happy smile. "Well, I've got a new uniform," I replied smugly, not to be outdone.

One evening David was getting ready to take a bath. He was eight now and had begun to attend the junior boy's school, which was on the other side of the infant school in Pelham Road. As he removed his vest, I heard my mother gasp.

"Arthur," she called. "Come and look at his back."

Of course, we all came running to see what she had seen. David had long red wheals across his back. "What happened to your back?" Daddy asked. David began to cry, thinking he was in trouble. "I got the cane. Mr. Nottle hit me," he said between sobs.

Mr. Nottle was David's new teacher. The next day Daddy went to the school with David to report what had happened to the headmaster and to show him what this teacher had done to his son.

David had a tendency, like me, to go into a dreamy state and would stare out of the window. As he wasn't paying attention to the lesson, Mr. Nottle had beaten him with his cane. It transpired that this teacher lost his teaching job at the school when they discovered that David was not the only child to suffer at his hands.

Poor David, he wasn't the only one to use daydreaming to escape from the effects of the war. Unfortunately, David had a teacher who would not tolerate it. Still, at least Daddy's action had saved some other poor boy from a beating!

One day Betty came home with a young man. His name was Robert Monk, and he was in the navy. When he came home on leave, Betty and Bob would sit gazing into one another's eyes, looking, I thought, very soppy.

Betty's friend, Peggy Taylor, who lived in Woolwich Road, just around the corner from us, was sweet on Robert's brother, Charley, and the four of them would go out on dates together.

It wasn't long before Betty and Robert decided to marry. Betty came home, her eyes shining. "We are engaged," she said happily, "Robert has asked me to marry him!"

My parents were not happy as the couple had decided to marry in a registry office, instead of a church. I didn't get to go to the wedding, but we held the reception at our house. To accommodate the guests, we found another table to add to our dining table. Robert's mother (his father having died in the war) and some of his large family joined us as we squeezed into our small dining room. I don't remember much about the wedding or the reception.

Afterwards, Betty went to live with Robert at his mother's house, which was a small terraced house. Robert's house was of a similar style to the one in Padiham where Thelma and I had stayed during our evacuation, except that they had an inside loo. It was in Bexleyheath Broadway, just opposite the Police Station.

With Betty married and now gone, it meant that I was able to sleep with Sheila and Thelma in the double bed in their room. As I was now growing up, Mummy thought it would be much better for me, for which indeed it was, albeit a bit of a squeeze. Goodness knows how Sheila, Betty and Thelma slept in a double bed with so little room. At least now it wouldn't be such a squeeze on weekdays when Sheila wasn't there. Just a bit tight when Sheila would come home from the farm at weekends. With this change, now David could move into the other back bedroom with Brian.

Wendy, Brian and Thelma, with Mummy looking out of the window. Circa 1948

After Betty and Robert's Wedding, Peggy (Betty's friend from Woolwich Rd) and Charley (Robert's brother) got married the following Saturday at Christ Church. Betty again donned her wedding outfit, a powder blue coat and a small matching hat with a short veil. It looked beautiful against her fantastic auburn hair. In contrast, Robert donned his dark blue wedding suit. Betty and Robert had not been able to afford a wedding photographer, and so, cannily, they got Peggy and Charlie's photographer to take a picture of them outside the Church. Betty would have loved to have worn a long white dress when she got married, but money was tight, and so it was out of the question.

Within the year, 'Robert junior' arrived. He was a large baby, and Betty adored him. When they came to visit us, I was allowed to hold him, but as he grew older, he would grab my hair and scream. It was quite painful to extricate his little fingers from my long locks. I don't know why he did it. I always tried to stay away from him after that first time. His fascination for my hair scared me.

8

A HOLIDAY ON MY OWN

MUMMY HAD THREE SISTERS STILL LIVING. SHE HAD BEEN ONE OF twelve children; nine girls and three boys. They had grown up in a large Victorian house in New Cross. Two of Mummy's sisters had died when the Spanish Flu pandemic hit in 1918.

The second eldest sister, Lily, now lived in a bungalow in Tankerton, Kent, with Percy, her husband, one son and a daughter, Alan and Rona. Sadly, Lily's other son, Dennis, had been a pilot in the war. He lost his life at age twenty-two, while on a night run.

Mummy's eldest sister was Flora. She had lived with her husband Arthur, and one son and daughter, Geoffrey and Joyce, in Lea-on-Sea Essex. Flora had been very feisty and had joined the suffragette movement in her youth. I heard that she had even chained herself to some railings. Daddy used to say she was bossy as she was always telling him what to do.

The third sister I had met was Marie. She had been christened Gertrude Marie but didn't like the name Gertrude, so she decided to be known as just plain Marie. Daddy used to say, “Her name is Gertrude, but we call her Gert and leave out the rude part!”

Marie also lived in Tankerton. She lived in a bungalow with her elderly husband, Gerald. Gerald was related to the Cruft family of ‘Crufts Dog Show’ fame. They met when Marie was nursing him in the hospital. He now used a wheelchair after having suffered a stroke.

One day my mother received a letter from her sister, Marie, and on opening it she exclaimed,

“Oh, it's from Auntie Gertie,” she said, smiling. “She wants to know if you would like to go and stay with her and your Uncle for Easter.”

“Oh, can I, please?”

I was thrilled when my parents agreed for me to travel by myself on the Green-Line bus, to be met at the other end by my Aunt. Mummy had shown me a picture of my Auntie Marie so that I would recognize her when I saw her. I was to travel in the School holidays on the Wednesday before Easter.

When the day arrived, Mummy and I set off to the Green Line bus stop near the clock tower, outside Mence Smith, the ironmongers. I carried a small case of clothes, and a jam sandwich in a brown paper bag for the journey. As the coach arrived, I climbed in while my mother paid the driver, informing him that I would be met at the other end. Then she handed me the ticket, “Don’t lose it, and don’t talk to strangers,” she warned. She gave me a final hug and a kiss. The folding door closed, and we were off!

I felt slightly scared; it was the first time I had travelled alone. I decided to ignore everyone else, and instead, I gazed out of the windows watching the world go by. The rocking of the coach made me nod off, and when I awoke, it was to the sight of miles and miles of fruit trees in pink and white blossom. Running between the trees frolicked new-born lambs. I thought to myself, 'How white they are, compared to the mother sheep who were brown and dirty.' I gazed at them, fascinated.

During the journey, the orchards gave way to the hop fields and the towering wooden frames ready to carry the ever-climbing hop plants. In the summer, hordes of families, mostly from the East end of London, would descend on the fields to pick the hops, which were made into good Kentish ale. I was beginning to feel hungry by now, and I reached into my bag for my jam sandwich. It was somewhat squashed, but I relished it anyway, licking the jam off my fingers. My gaze turned again to the window and there, in the distance, I could see the sea.

I thrilled at the now-familiar sight and became excited at the thought of being on holiday by myself, without my brothers and sisters. I remembered my last holiday with the family at Camber Sands and the fun Brian and I had on the dunes. I had always been surrounded by my brothers and sisters wherever I went, so this was a new adventure for me.

The coach eventually arrived at Tankerton, and as we pulled up at the seafront, there was my Aunt ready to meet me, together with my Uncle in his wheelchair. I recognized her straight away and waved to them as I hurriedly jumped down the steps of the coach. I then stood feeling shy, as my Aunt made her way towards me.

A robust offshore wind tugged at my coat. Auntie Marie gave me a hug and then, holding me at arm's length, she admired my coat and woolly Juliet bonnet that Thelma had made me. The hat was made from pink angora and had bobbles all over it. I loved wearing it. The knitting pattern had been so popular that everywhere you went, you would see girls and young women wearing these hats. A plastic Alice band was threaded through the edge to hold it to your head. The angora felt so soft and kept my head warm.

Taking hold of my bag, Auntie Marie gazed at me and introduced me to Uncle, who grunted, "hello." Auntie exclaimed, "My, haven't you grown! It's lovely to see you, at last. Come along, this way; it isn't far to walk." I hadn't remembered my Aunt ever seeing me before, so how did she know I had grown? But I figured that maybe my mother had sent her photos of me.

Auntie Marie was a little taller than I, with dark wavy hair, cut short. I trotted obediently beside her as she pushed Uncle in the wheelchair along the road, which led us away from the seafront. We passed rows of bungalows, their front gardens aglow with yellow daffodils, red tulips, and purple aubrietia. I loved seeing those colours together. Occasionally we came across a pink almond tree in blossom. I gazed around at the colourful gardens in the bright sunshine and their spring finery. I breathed in deeply, "ah!" The fresh aroma of spring, mixed with the salty air coming off the sea, it was as good as a tonic.

It seemed an age to me before we finally stood before my Aunt's bungalow, though in reality, we had walked barely half a mile. Her home was positioned on a corner and boasted a sizeable, colourful garden on two sides, with a pond at the back. We walked up the garden path, and Auntie Marie opened the front door. Then lifting the wheels of Uncle's invalid chair, we went inside.

Through the front door was a narrow hall with rooms leading off it. First, a bedroom on the right, then straight ahead was the lounge. We turned left, and on the left side, just around the corner, was my bedroom. Auntie placed my case on the bed and pointed to the chest of drawers and a standing wardrobe.

"You can put your clothes in there. I will settle Uncle first, it is time for his nap. The bathroom is the next room along if you need it," She added.

While Auntie Marie made Uncle comfortable in his bed, I looked around my room. The curtains at the window caught my eye first. They were a colourful chintz fabric. Then, I noticed the green satin eiderdown that covered the bed.

I walked to the window, narrowly missing a vase of mixed daffodils, narcissus, and sprigs of pussy willow. Their beautiful scent was filling the room. Stroking the softness of the grey buds on the willow, I gazed out of the window. A flowering cherry tree grew outside. Each pink blossom, with the stamens covered in yellow pollen looking like a fairy crown. They looked so pretty up close.

My Aunt returned, and she helped me to put away my clothes. She said, "Come with me, and I will show you around, it is going to be so nice having you to stay." She added with a smile.

First, she showed me the bathroom that was next to my bedroom. The door opposite was Auntie and Uncle's bedroom. Near the front door, was yet another bedroom and a large lounge with a bay window. The lounge had a fireplace and on the mantle stood a sizeable ornate clock under a glass dome. Two cherubs swung to and fro as the pendulum. I gazed at it with great interest.

For seating, they had a three-piece suite that was arranged invitingly in front of the fire. In the corner on one side was a tea trolley with a starched white embroidered tray cloth. On the other side stood an exquisite coffee table, next to that was a glass cabinet filled with all manner of bric-a-brac.

My Aunt showed me the kitchen at the end of the hall. It stretched the whole width of the bungalow. Through an open door that led into the dining room, I saw that a highly polished dark oak table was set ready for tea. This room, like the kitchen, stretched the width of the bungalow with French doors leading out into the garden. On the sideboard stood a large silver tray with a gleaming silver tea service. I was amazed; it was something I had never before seen. There was a strong smell of lavender wax polish, and the furniture shone with the care that my Aunt had so obviously lavished upon it.

"It's time for tea," Auntie announced, and taking the silver teapot from the tray, carried it into the kitchen.

I followed behind her feeling very hungry, and watched as she filled the kettle and placing it on the stove, she lit the gas. It was a whistling kettle, and it was soon singing away merrily.

My Aunt pointed to some cake tins. "You can put the cakes out, Wendy," she said, handing me a tiered cake stand to arrange them on. I opened one tin filled with cream cakes and chocolate éclairs. The next tin had a large Madeira cake with slices of lemon baked into the top. Auntie Marie beamed at me, "I baked them, especially for your visit," she said proudly.

I felt very honoured as I carefully carried the cakes into the dining room. Where the table, covered with a pure white starched linen cloth, was topped with fine bone china plates. My Aunt then carried both the teapot and a plate of thin cucumber sandwiches with the crusts removed. We sat down as Auntie placed the teapot back on the silver tray. I noticed a starched white linen serviette beside my plate rolled up and placed inside a silver serviette ring. I keenly observed as my Aunt took her serviette from its collar. Leaving the ring beside her plate, she put the serviette carefully in her lap, so, anxious to please her, I did the same.

I soon learned that this was a daily ritual, and under my Aunt's guidance, I learned how to set the table properly. My Uncle didn't join us on this occasion as the walk to fetch me from the bus had tired him out. I ate several cucumber sandwiches hungrily, it seemed ages since I had eaten my brown-bagged sandwich on the bus. My Aunt's cakes looked much too good to *not* try.

The taste matched the look, they were simply delicious, and the lemon Madeira was so light. Auntie Marie was as excellent a cook as my mother. I wondered if she also owned Mrs. Beeton's Cookery Book.

"On Good Friday, we will go to church," Auntie Marie announced. "You do go to church, don't you?" She asked, hopefully. I nodded, my mouth full of cake. "Yes, I have been going to church and Sunday school ever since I could walk, and before that, I was put on the church's 'cradle roll.' We go to the Congregational Church, at the end of Chapel Road opposite the Palace Cinema." I continued. "Sometimes, we all go, but more often than not, just Thelma, Brian and I go to Sunday school."

We finished tea, and I helped my Aunt clear the table and wash the dishes. Seeing me gazing through the French windows, she said to me, "Would you like to come and see the garden?" I smiled and nodded; nothing would delight me more.

My Aunt led me through the French doors leading from the dining room. The garden was full of waving daffodils and pale narcissus, bright red and soft pink tulips and carpets of purple aubrietia. There were two apple trees in blossom and a small lawn surrounded with the overflowing flowerbeds. The sun felt warm on my back as I bent to smell the flowers.

Next, Auntie showed me the pond. It was brimming with the jelly-like eggs of frogspawn, and inside the egg sacks, the tiny dots of tadpoles were starting to wriggle, longing to be free to explore their world. Auntie fetched a small fishing net on a long cane, and together we fished some of the frogspawn out, carefully putting it into a jam jar. Auntie added a piece of pondweed so that the tadpoles had something to cling to once they had hatched. "Otherwise, they will sink to the bottom," she explained. I was so enthralled by the tiny creatures and was allowed to carry the jar indoors and place it on the kitchen windowsill, at the same time making sure it wasn't in the sun. "We don't want to cook them," Auntie smiled.

Each day I would gaze into the jar, and gradually the tadpoles hatched. I watched, enthralled, as they grew from a black dot, to an oval with a tail. First, their back legs appeared and then the front ones. When they got to that stage, Auntie made me put them back in the pond. She said she didn't want to wake up in the morning and find the kitchen full of frogs! I was reluctant to release them. I found them so very fascinating to watch.

The following morning was raining, so Auntie found a jigsaw for Uncle and me to do together. We balanced it on a tray on Uncle's lap, but he soon grew tired of doing it and fell asleep, so I took the tray and carried it over to the sofa. I sat down with it, balanced on my knees. The picture was of a thatched country cottage with roses and hollyhocks around the door. It kept me completely engrossed until Auntie came in with a pot of coffee and placed it on the tea trolley.

"Time for our elevenses, could you help me with the tray. Please, Wendy?" she asked me. Being so eager to help, I jumped up and tipped the jigsaw pieces all over the carpet. I went very pink.

"Don't worry, dear," Auntie said kindly, "it won't take a minute to pick them up." And so she joined me on my knees, and we crawled around the floor until we had retrieved every piece. Auntie put them back into the box. “You can start it again this afternoon,” she told me, “now let's have our coffee.”

I helped her with the tray of cups and a plate of digestive biscuits to go with our coffee. “Oh, good,” mumbled Uncle Gerald, “They’re my favourite,” and he smiled affectionately at Auntie. I wasn’t used to drinking coffee – well, not proper coffee - as this was. We only had Camp coffee out of the bottle at home. This coffee was made like tea, in a special coffee pot. I took a sip. “Mmm. It is very nice,” I said, “I like it better than Camp coffee,” my Aunt laughed. “I should hope so,” she remarked, “I think there is no comparison. Camp coffee is a liquid containing flavourings while this coffee is made with freshly roasted coffee beans.” So as not to show my ignorance, I kept silent. I didn’t know that coffee came from beans as far as I knew, it came in a bottle.

On Good Friday morning, I awoke once more to the sound of a blackbird singing for joy in the cherry tree outside my window. I lay in bed for a while, gazing at the patterns on the chintz curtains. I had a lovely cozy feeling, and I loved this bedroom. It was so lovely to have a room of my own for once and not to have my sisters’ elbows or knees sticking into me. To have such undivided attention from Auntie was a real bonus.

A gentle tap at the door heralded the arrival of Auntie Marie, carrying a cup of tea with two digestive biscuits in the saucer. Such luxury!

She drew the curtains, and the sun streamed in at the window. “Good morning Wendy. Get up and have a wash, then we will have breakfast,” she announced.

By the time I had finished my tea and biscuits, washed and dressed and combed my hair, the incredible smell of frying bacon and eggs had permeated the air.

I wandered into the kitchen just as my Aunt was loading the plates with the lovely thick bacon and eggs with golden yellow centres. The delicious smell of the food made my mouth water. Auntie turned as I entered and smiled a welcome. "You go and sit up and keep Uncle company."

I went through into the dining room where my Uncle Gerald was sitting at the table in his wheelchair. I smiled at him shyly. "Good morning, my dear," he smiled back at me, "Happy Easter." His words were slurred as a result of the stroke he had suffered, and I found it hard to understand him. Yet, I returned his greeting.

My Aunt came in, carrying a tray with a toast rack of toast and a twin eggcup with two brown eggs. She placed it in front of Uncle, who was sitting patiently, his serviette tucked into his necktie. "I gave them four minutes, just as you like them," she announced, placing the eggs in front of Uncle.

She disappeared into the kitchen again. She returned carrying a tray with two plates of bacon, eggs, mushrooms and half a tomato.

I remembered to use my napkin, and after putting it in my lap, I delved into the bacon and eggs. I ate hungrily, finishing my meal with toast and homemade lemon jelly marmalade, delicious!

"You were hungry," Auntie observed as she lovingly wiped my Uncle's chin for him with his serviette. Seeing me looking, she explained. "Uncle has lost the feeling in his face, so he doesn't know when he has food on his chin."

"All right, all right," Uncle said crossly, "she doesn't need to know that." My Aunt fell silent.

After breakfast, it was time to go to church. We set out together, with my Aunt again pushing the wheelchair. I am sure Uncle was no lightweight, but she didn't complain. She wrapped a tartan blanket around his legs; it was still quite fresh as the wind was again coming off the sea. There was a smell of salt in the air.

The sun was shining on the golden daffodils nodding their heads in the breeze that accompanied us as we wandered along the lane. The birds were noisily singing as we reached the old stone church.

We entered through the Norman style arched door and sat down in a hard wooden pew, halfway along. My Aunt settled Uncle into his seat and then took his wheelchair to the back of the church. I looked around and marvelled at the stone carvings that decorated the nave. Auntie had removed the embroidered cassock that hung on a hook on the pew in front and signalled to me to do the same. As we both knelt in prayer, our heads bowed on our hands; I wasn't sure what to pray, so I thanked God for "bringing me here." As I sat back in my seat, I gazed around at the beautiful stained glass windows.

The service began with the Vicar welcoming us all, "On this lovely Easter Friday morning." We sang:

"There is a green hill far away outside a city wall,
Where the dear Lord was crucified, He died to
save us all.
We may not know we cannot tell what pain he had
to bear.
But we believe it was for us. He hung and suffered
there".

It made me very sad. Then the Vicar started his sermon; he began, "Dear Lord, we are all sinners,"

"What!" I thought, "I haven't sinned. I haven't stolen anything or killed anyone. I am certainly not a sinner!" I couldn't understand why he had included me. My mind went off at a tangent, and the Vicar's sermon faded away as I gazed around the church at the beautiful stained glass windows.

I looked across at my Aunt and Uncle. Auntie Marie was listening intently, but Uncle's head had dropped to his chest. He was asleep! My mind came back to the Vicar's sermon.

Finally, the minister concluded, "But our sins are forgiven because of the sacrifice Christ made for us on the Cross." "Oh, thank goodness," I thought, feeling relieved.

The service came to an end, and after placing Uncle Gerald back in his wheelchair, we emerged together with the rest of the congregation from the dim light of the church out into brilliant sunshine. The vicar stood at the entrance shaking hands with everyone as they left. Auntie introduced me, "This is my niece Wendy," she announced to him. "I'm very pleased to meet you," he said, shaking my hand warmly. "Do come again." I smiled shyly back at him, as he turned to the next parishioner.

We strolled back along the country lanes with the sun warm upon my back. By this time, I was beginning to feel hungry again and wondered what amazing things we would be having for dinner.

At last, we arrived back at the bungalow. I held the gate while Uncle was wheeled up the path, but as we opened the door, we were met with billowing smoke!

The whole house was full of black smoke coming from the front bedroom. The culprit was an oil heater, which had been left on to warm the home while we were at church. Auntie quickly turned it off, and I opened the windows.

We pulled the bedding off the bed and removed the curtains from the windows, throwing them into the laundry basket. My Aunt surveyed the damage, "Well, it might have been worse," she said with a wry smile.

Shutting the bedroom door, she went to rescue Uncle, who had been sitting helplessly in his chair outside. Seeing his worried expression as she settled him in the lounge, she said, "It's all right now, everything is under control. We need a cup of tea! Put the kettle on Wendy."

Later, when she was telling a friend about the fire, she praised my calmness and the way I went and opened the windows. "You would make a good nurse," she said. I beamed proudly in the light of her praise.

I learned a lot from my Aunt Marie. She taught me how to clean silver, and the correct way to set the table She taught me the best way to dust a room. "You start at the door and work your way around each piece of furniture polishing and dusting as you go," she told me. Soon I was cleaning her dining room like a professional cleaner. She showed me how to polish the furniture by taking a little of the wax onto the duster and rubbing in small circular movements. Then I was to rub it with a clean fluffy yellow duster until it shone. I loved making the wood shine, and I also loved the smell of the Lavender wax as I polished her beautiful table. It did not seem a chore to me; I felt honoured to be allowed to do it.

She taught me how to make a perfect cup of tea. "And when you make tea, you must always remember to warm the pot first. Put a spoonful of tea into the pot, one for each person and one for the pot, and pour the boiling water onto the tea while it is still boiling." She went on, "then you must wait four minutes for the tea to brew before you pour it, and always put the milk in the cup before you add the tea, so that the hot water doesn't crack the porcelain."

Auntie had a beautiful silver sugar bowl filled with sugar lumps and a little pair of silver sugar tongs. After tea, I had to brush the crumbs from the tablecloth with a small brush into a small silver pan made for the purpose. Auntie didn't do anything as 'vulgar' as shaking the cloth in the garden for the birds, the way we did at home. The table cloth was then folded neatly and put away in the drawer.

One day the postman arrived with a postcard from my mother. I picked up the card from the doormat and handed it to my Aunt, she read it and then exclaimed, "Fancy writing that for all the world to read, why couldn't she send me a letter?"

Handing it back to me, I read: - "I have bought Wendy a new liberty bodice so that you can use her old one for dusters." The liberty bodice was the white cotton garment I wore over my undervest for extra warmth. It had rubber buttons and attached suspenders to hold up my Lyle stockings. My Aunt was appalled that such an intimate garment should be discussed on a postcard! She was also amazed that my mother should consider using it as a duster. After all, her dusters were all fluffy and yellow and made for the job.

Auntie Marie was still going on about my liberty bodice as we went out to visit my Mother's second eldest sister, Lily. She lived a few streets away in a beautiful bungalow that had an Inglenook fireplace in the living room. Auntie Lily was tall and willowy. "She wrote it on a postcard!" Auntie relayed the story again to my Auntie Lily, who simply smiled. Auntie Lily, my Uncle Percy and her son Alan were at home. Her daughter Rona was at work.

Uncle Percy had been in the Cavalry when he was younger, and two of his dress swords hung above the fireplace. Along the mantle beam below were several shiny horse-brasses. Small seats were positioned on both sides of the fire. The seats had little alcoves containing shiny brass ornaments.

The windows of the bungalow had latticed glass, and the living room was beautifully decorated with dark oak beams and shiny furniture like Auntie Marie's. She also had chintz curtains hanging at the windows.

Auntie Lily was wearing a scarf, tied back behind her head to protect her hair and an apron. Obviously, she had been busy cleaning the living room before we arrived. Quickly removing the telltale garments, Auntie Lily hugged me and said, "Lovely to see you, won't you come into the garden?" To Auntie Marie, she said, "Isn't she like Doris," referring to my mother.

With Auntie Lily leading the way, we went through the open French doors to the garden. My Uncle Percy was reading the newspaper, sitting at a small table surrounded by deck chairs. As we approached, he folded the paper, stood and shook my hand.

"Isn't she like Doris," he remarked, looking me over.

"The garden is looking nice," said Auntie Marie, changing the subject. "Come and see, Wendy."

I followed my two Aunts around the garden. The long flower borders had scalloped edges and were edged alternately with white alyssum and mauve aubrietia. At the end of the garden was a small group of blossoming fruit trees with clumps of daffodils growing amongst them.

I stood and gazed at the flowers, lost in thought. I thought it was an excellent idea to make the flower borders scalloped instead of straight, like ours at home, until Auntie Lily's voice broke into my thoughts. "Come and have some tea!" She called.

Turning, I noticed the garden table was laid with a white linen table cloth. There were sandwiches and cakes on plates lined with doilies. My Aunt had honoured us with her best bone china tea service. Like Auntie Marie, Auntie Lily had made wafer-thin cucumber sandwiches cut into quarters and with the crusts removed. It appeared it was the thing to do.

I ate hungrily, finishing off with an iced fairy cake. "Have another cake," Auntie Lily offered the plate. "No, thank you," I answered politely, "I'm TTT." My Aunt looked puzzled. "Tummy touching table!" I explained. "That's not very ladylike," Auntie Marie said, disapprovingly.

Uncle Percy slapped his thigh and roared with laughter. "Oh, leave the girl alone," he said, as he winked at me. I smiled sheepishly as Auntie Lily refilled his teacup for the third time. By the time we left, Uncle and I were firm friends.

The next day, Auntie Marie announced that we were going on a trip to Canterbury to see the Cathedral. I was very excited at the thought of just the two of us going on a trip. My Aunt had arranged for a neighbour to sit in with Uncle while we were away. "He will be fine with my friend Joan," she said, adding with a smile, "She trained as a nurse with me."

The weather looked fair, and the temperature seemed to be rising. Auntie had a barometer in her hall, and she always gave it a tap before we went out. I decided to wear my green cotton skirt with the coloured pansies embroidered on the straps that Thelma had made for me. I would also wear my white cotton blouse with the Peter Pan collar, together with my short white socks and brown sandals. Auntie made me put on a cardigan, "Just in case," she said. "The wind can still be quite chilly, and we don't want you catching a cold."

We caught the bus at the top of the road, and I sat next to Auntie and gazed out of the window as she pointed out various places of interest to me.

My Aunt had decided that we would stop off at a little village called Harbledown for some lunch before we went into Canterbury. As we alighted from the bus, I looked around. The town was like something from a storybook. All the houses and cottages had thatched roofs; even the bus shelter was thatched.

As we walked along the road, I gazed at the beautiful sight of the brightly coloured gardens. They reminded me of Auntie's jigsaw puzzle. I was enthralled at such a pretty place. Auntie Marie smiled as she saw my face, "I knew you would like it!" she told me.

We found a tiny tearoom and went in. The square tables were set with flower-sprigged tablecloths and small vases of wildflowers. Sitting down at a table near the window, Auntie ordered some egg and cress sandwiches, and a pot of tea. When they arrived, I tucked in hungrily. My Aunt poured the tea, plopping two sugar lumps into each cup, then the milk and finally the tea. The waitress brought us a cake stand full of little iced and cream cakes, together with slices of fruitcake. I chose a pink iced butterfly cake (the top had been sliced off, cut in half then arranged on the top of the iced cupcake to look like butterfly wings.) Then I also had a chocolate éclair stuffed with cream, after having waited to see which cake Auntie Marie chose to have. I had wanted to take the éclair as soon as I saw it, but remembered my manners and let Auntie choose first. She had been watching my face also and was well aware of which cake I wanted. She smiled to herself as I finally reached for the éclair, pleased that I had remembered my manners.

"Do you know how Harbledown got its name?" Auntie asked me, knowing full well that I didn't. I shook my head. "Well," she went on without waiting for an answer, "King Henry 2nd walked barefoot through Harbledown on a Pilgrimage to Canterbury Cathedral in repentance. He was sorry for his mistaken involvement in the murder of Thomas Becket. So they called the place Hobbledown, and later it became known as Harbledown. "Oh. Who is Thomas Bucket?" I asked.

"No," corrected my Aunt, "Thomas Becket or Thomas-a-Becket, as he was sometimes called, was the Archbishop of Canterbury, in the year 1162." "Well, that was a very long time ago, wasn't it?" I said as I digested what she had told me. We finished our meal, Auntie paid the bill, and we left the tearoom.

We walked a little further and admiring more of the darling thatched cottages and their colourful gardens. We made our way back to the bus stop to continue our journey to Canterbury. The sun was brightly shining as we reached the old town, and my Aunt pointed out the ancient flint wall that still surrounded the city. "This wall dates back to the twelfth century," she reminded me. "And it is still standing after all those years," I added, impressed.

The Cathedral was huge and very imposing, and as we went through the arched doorway into the coolness of the inside, I gazed at the high vaulted ceilings and beautiful stone carving. Auntie and I walked around for a while, admiring the architecture. I could hear singing, and Auntie led me to where the choir was beginning evensong. We sat down on some chairs to listen.

The young choirboys looked lovely in their white robes and high frilly collars, and I was amazed at their voices. I don't think I had ever heard anything so pleasant as the sound that echoed around the Cathedral.

I took in the beautiful stained glass windows. One circular window was especially stunning. So, too were the remarkable thirteenth century carved arches and high ceiling. I was amazed at this place and how old it all was. As I took in the ancient tombs, I wondered to myself about Thomas-a-Becket, murdered there so long ago. My Aunt showed me the steps upon which he had been murdered and told me how he had suffered from wearing the rough hair shirt he wore under his robes. After his murder, it was discovered that his shirt was infested with fleas! Eeuw!

We explored the town with its ancient buildings, narrow streets and fascinating shops. I bought a postcard with a picture of the Cathedral on it to send home to Mummy and Daddy, before we boarded the bus back to Tankerton. It was time to leave.

After arriving back at my Aunt's bungalow, I was bursting with all the news to tell Uncle. "And do you know, Uncle, the Cathedral is so old! And Thomas-a-Becket was murdered there!" My words tumbled out, and Uncle Gerald chuckled at my enthusiasm.

I spent the rest of my vacation going to the beach, paddling in the sea and collecting seashells. We also went for a visit into Whitstable one day, and I watched the men digging for mussels on the seashore.

I was busy helping my Aunt each day with her chores and managing Uncle. Before I left, Auntie Marie lowered the ladder that led to the attic rooms and allowed me to climb up with her. From the treasures she kept there, she found and gifted me a small Japanese porcelain vase, and two silver serving spoons. We wrapped them carefully in a newspaper, and I put them in my bag.

When it was time to leave, I kissed and hugged and said my goodbyes to my Aunt and Uncle before boarding the waiting bus. I waved to them both until they were out of sight. What a lovely time I had had, I smiled to myself at the memories.

As the bus rattled along the country lanes of Kent, I recalled all that I had seen and done with my Auntie Marie. I was going to miss her, and her way of life. I had grown quite attached to Auntie Marie and to having so much attention paid to me. Now it was back to the old familiar surroundings, Mummy and Daddy and the rest of the family; it was also time to go back to school.

9

ANOTHER NEW SCHOOL

Now that the school holidays were over, it was time for yet another change in my life. A new school.

It seemed strange to be attending yet another new school, and this time it was a girls-only school. Although my last school was mostly girls, boys were allowed to participate for the first year, before they moved on.

In this school, the teachers were strict. We had to change classrooms for each lesson. I now had homework, and the lessons, of course, had become harder. Having missed so much schooling because of my asthma and the air raids during the war, I was hopeless at maths. Although Daddy tried to help me with it, it was utterly alien to me; I didn't get it.

My new teacher, Miss Gain, didn't help. She made me stand out in front of the class and try to work out a problem on the blackboard. I was timid and confused, and the rest of the girls laughed at me. It was like a foreign language to me; I did not know what she meant. I did not like Miss Gain, and I don't think she thought much of me either. Miss Gain also taught music, in the music room, pounding on the piano while we sang,

"Once there was a dragon dressed in green
All in green, all in green,
Never has a worse one yet been seen,
Than the dragon who was dressed in green.
Envious and spiteful is his name
Dreadful name
Dragon's name
Envious and spiteful is his name.
The dragon who is dressed in green.
Should you ever meet him,
As you may, one fine day
Far away,
Should you ever meet him
You must slay
The dragon who is dressed in green.
Once there was a dragon dressed in red
All in red all in red
Never has a worse one yet been fed
Than the dragon who is dressed in red....etc.,

Then:-

Once there was a dragon dressed in black
All in black all in black
Never has a worse one crossed your track
Than the dragon who is dressed in black.
Gloomy and revengeful is his name
Dreadful name, dragon's name
Gloomy and revengeful is his name
The dragon who is dressed in black."

Should you ever meet him…

"Sing out, girls! Sing out!" Miss Gain would shout above the din. She loved that song.

She also loved us to sing sea shanties.

"Oh, Shenandoah, I love your daughter,
A-way you rolling river…

In class, I sat next to a freckle-faced girl named Eileen Hullet. She would pinch me and give me what was described as a 'Chinese burn' on my wrist. This was achieved by taking hold of a wrist with both hands and twisting the skin in opposite directions. It would burn! I tried not to show any emotion as she did it. I hoped that she would soon stop, and dreaded having to go to school each day and sit next to her. It never occurred to me to tell someone what was happening to me, day after day. Finally, she got tired of assaulting me, and we became friends.

I learned that her older brother used to do the same to her, so I suppose she had to get her own back somehow, and I just happened to be there. However, she was quite impressed that I didn't cry or yell when she did it, as she knew first hand just how much it hurt.

During P.E. (physical education) and games lessons, our class was divided into different 'houses.' Each 'house' was named after a famous woman. To identify girls from each 'house,' we wore coloured bands across our chests.

There was a "Nightingale" house named after the nurse, Florence Nightingale. The pupils in that house wore dark blue bands. "Cavell" House, named after Edith Cavell, another famous nurse. The colour of their group was green. Then there was "Fry" house after Elizabeth Fry, the Quaker prison reformer, they wore red bands. The final colour was yellow for “Anderson” House named after Elizabeth Garret Anderson, the first woman physician. I was in “Cavell” House with a green band.

“House Points” were awarded to the winners of the games we played. We could also gain and lose house points with the way we behaved and how well or poorly we did our lessons. At the end of term, on sports day, we competed against each other. All the points were added to find the winner.

At school, one lesson I did enjoy was Nature Study. I became close friends with Dawn Loft. I was allowed to go to her house after school, and we would wander around her garden collecting things like bird’s nests, leaves, flowers, and interesting rocks. We made a nature table in her bedroom to display all the amazing things we had found until her mother made us clear it all away. I could never understand why she didn’t see these things as exciting as we did.

I also made friends with a pretty girl called Marjorie Button; she had lovely thick blonde wavy hair. Marjorie lived in Long Lane, and I was invited to tea several times. I was a giggler then, and so was she, so we had lots of fun together. My Daddy used to call me “Giggling Gertie.”

We had an extensive library at the Central School, and I would take out books on plants and read them over and over, learning their common names and botanical names in Latin. I would draw pictures of plants in a notebook and study them. I had also become intrigued with books on historical costume through the ages and would gaze, fascinated at the illustrations. I wished we wore crinolines, like the Victorians, or beautiful Edwardian creations with high necks and leg-of-mutton-sleeves, or even some of the long flowing dresses, I saw in these pictures. They were so much prettier than our clothes.

I tried my hand at designing dresses, sketching in my notebook. My designs were very strange, though not unlike some fashions one sees today in fashion shows from America and Paris.

I realized that I enjoyed drawing. I can remember filling a whole book with little ballerina figures in different poses, wearing tutus, all with pointed toes in ballet shoes. I can remember when I was staying with Auntie Marie, showing her, and she thought they were "awfully good."

Dancing was also still of great interest to me, and I joined in with a group of older girls, practicing tap dancing on the school field during the lunch break. It was rather hard to dance on the grass, but I managed to learn the "time step", though I nearly always became too breathless to dance for any length of time.

An older girl called Pamela Watson would grab me and hug me. I think that as I was small for my age, she felt as though she wanted to mother me. I remember that she had a rather ample bosom, and it embarrassed me so much when she hugged me that in the end, I left the group. However, I still used to practice dancing at home on the concrete strip in the garden outside the kitchen.

Our school field was adjacent to the boy's school field of Graham Road Boys School, with a path separating the two high wire fences. Some of the girls would exchange notes with the boys by wrapping them around stones and throwing them over these fences. The footpath that ran between them was the one I took each day from Pelham Road to school. It led to Belvedere Road and then on to Church Road, where my last school was. So I didn't have to walk quite so far to this school. I could not understand the interest in boys. To me, at this time in my life, they were both noisy and dirty.

One day Mummy asked me to go shopping for her. "Could you go to the Co-op and get me some white tape? Then, if you cross the road, you can get some cakes from Goodfare's the bakers," she instructed. So I took the money and the shopping bag my Mother handed to me and started my journey towards the clock tower. From the clock tower, I wandered down the Broadway, looking in the shop windows. Next door to the bakers was a toy shop. I looked in the window and then entered the shop to look around.

I had some of my pocket money with me. Daddy gave us "Saturday Money" as we called it, each week if we had been good and helped Mummy. As I looked around the shop, my gaze fell on a small doll, about 10 inches long. She was plastic with moving legs and arms and had blonde hair. There was also a dark-haired one. They were Rosebud dolls and thinking back, they must have been the precursor of the Barbie doll, although their bodies were straight up and down, unlike Barbie's curvy one.

I looked at the price. It was one shilling and sixpence, which was more than the Saturday money I had, so I decided to return the next week when I would have some more money with me. I left the shop and crossed the road to the Co-op. It was quite a large store. I went in and saw that the counter with the tape was at the far end. I walked to the counter and purchased two yards of the white tape that Mummy needed. As the assistant cut the required length and wrapped it up, she gave me my change along with the white slip of paper that I had to exchange for metal tokens at the small window as I went out. If we had saved enough metal tokens, they could be exchanged for merchandise. Stuffing the slip of paper in my pocket together with my change, I promptly forgot about the metal tokens and left the shop to buy the cakes that Mummy had asked me to get.

I crossed the busy road and went into Goodfares. I purchased a dozen fancy cakes. As I handed the woman the money, I suddenly remembered the slip of paper I still had in my pocket from the Co-op. I realized that if I didn't change it that day, it would be invalid, so I went to cross the road between two parked cars. I did not notice the car that hit me.

I screamed, and as I lost consciousness, my shopping bag fell on the road beside me. I came around to find someone carrying me and placing me into a borrowed chair from the cake shop, outside of the shop. Lots of people gathered around me, staring. My right arm and leg hurt and were bleeding. I tried to stand up, but I couldn't, so to remove me from the nosy crowd, someone else carried me into the cake shop, through another door and upstairs to a bedroom. I was laid on the bed while they bandaged my leg and arm.

Someone said, "The ambulance is on its way. What is your name, and where do you live?"

I tried to sit up, I wanted to go home, but there was no way they would allow me to leave. When the ambulance arrived, I was lifted onto a stretcher, together with my now rather battered shopping. I was assured that my parents would be informed that they were taking me to the Cottage Hospital to be examined by a doctor.

Sitting up in a hospital bed, after being examined by the doctor, with fresh dressings put on my arm and leg, I was told that I was well enough to go home.

I felt much better and able to joke to the nurse. “How high is a Chinaman?” I said. The nurse frowned, thinking I must have hit my head. “Well, that depends,” she answered slowly. “No,” I said, “that is his name - HowHi!” At that moment, Daddy came into the ward. “You can take her home,” the nurse smiled. “She is well enough to tell jokes.”

Back home the next day, we had a visit from the driver of the car who had hit me. I was resting in bed, so Mummy brought him upstairs to see me. As it happened, he had no car insurance, so he was in trouble. But he was happy that I was alright and he bought me a gold cross and chain to make up for knocking me down, I still have it.

Rosina Brett, Joyce Smith, Dawn Loft, Sylvia Dingley and myself decided to form a club. Rosina lived around the corner from me in Erith Road. It was at the far end of my road past the allotments and beyond the bus depot. On Tuesday evenings we would all meet at her house. Her mother allowed us to hold our meetings in their garden shed, so we made it our clubhouse.

Sometimes we were allowed into her kitchen, and Rosina’s Mother would patiently show us how to cook. I can remember her teaching us how to make apple dumplings and how surprised Mummy was when I arrived home with two huge dumplings wrapped in a tea towel. I was very proud of them, and they were delicious.

I felt that my mother seemed older than my friend’s mothers and I can remember being told by Rosina’s brother Raymond, when he came to call for me, “Your Grandmother opened the door.” I was mortified and told him it was my mother, but he insisted it was my Grandmother until I told him I didn't have one. Mummy was fifty-one at this time, but she appeared older, which was not surprising having brought up seven children, and with her health not being at all good.

I remember that the doctor had wanted her to have some special treatment for her asthma, but she refused, "I'm not going to be a guinea pig." she would say. So she continued to take the Ephedrine Hydrochloride tablets or "asthma tablets" as she called them.

One day at the end of April, I picked some May blossom off the tree outside the school on my way home. I proudly presented the boughs of sweet-smelling white blossom to my mother, thinking she would be pleased. Instead, she turned pale and flung it out into the garden. "It is very unlucky to bring May blossom into the house," she cried, with a look of horror on her face. "Don't ever do it again!" I was stunned. I didn't know about this belief, and I wondered if it were true.

One day, Sheila bought home a puppy. "He's a cross between a Labrador, Retriever and an Airedale," she told us. "You mean a Heinz 57," Daddy joked, "He is a mongrel." Sheila insisted that he wasn't a mongrel, "I have named him Gyp," she said, as we all gathered round to stroke and pat the small creature. He was cute, black with a brown face, and a black spot over each eye. He licked my hand and wagged his tail as I gingerly patted his small head.

I think Christopher grew closest to our dog. Once Gyp had grown, he would dress him up in an old Macintosh coat and tie him to his cart, then lead him up the garden path like a horse. Gyp loved

Christopher, and would even allow this small boy to ride on his back. We never managed to train Gyp to walk correctly on his lead, though, and whenever I took him to the park, he would bounce up and down all the way there.

Thelma wanted to practice her sewing techniques, and so she made two beautiful dresses for Mummy, they went to "Hides" and chose the fabric together. One of the materials was navy cloth, and the other was in grey. Thelma made Mummy some beautiful dresses. She was so happy to have something she was rarely, if ever, able to indulge in. She was looking forward to wearing them. They were hanging on the back of the bathroom door, waiting for Thelma to finish the hems, when we went shopping one day.

Unfortunately, someone had inadvertently shut Gyp in the bathroom. When we returned, the dresses were in tatters as Gyp had kept jumping up at the door to get out. Of course, we were all dreadfully upset for Mummy, but we couldn't be angry with Gyp, as he had only been trying to get out.

10

GOODBYE MUMMY

ONE DREARY DAY, WEDNESDAY THE 9TH OF MAY 1951. I WENT to school. Mummy had been sick all weekend, and so she had stayed in bed. Her asthma was becoming very noisy, and all she wanted to do was sleep. Daddy had asked the doctor to call in on Monday, but he hadn't yet arrived to see my mother. Daddy also asked Thelma to stay home from her job at Liberty's in Regent Street in the West End of London, where she worked as a seamstress. He asked her to look after Mummy while he went to work. I peaked in on my mother before I went to school. The bedroom curtains were drawn as she was still sleeping, so I didn't kiss her Good Bye as I didn't want to disturb her. I gently pulled the door closed, turned and tiptoed down the stairs. Little did I know, that I was to regret that decision for the rest of my life.

Thelma had made me some beef dripping and Marmite sandwiches for my lunch. I don't remember much about school that day, but by four o'clock, the time I had to leave, it had become very foggy.

I was used to taking the path across the fields past the cemetery, but I didn't fancy going that route in the fog. So instead, I went with a class chum Anne, the long way round, along Church Road and up the Broadway. We shared the dripping sandwiches that I hadn't eaten at break time. As we dawdled along, I can remember feeling worried and saying to her, "I have a funny feeling; I don't want to go home. I don't know why."

We continued on our journey until we parted company at Woolwich Road, and as I slowly wandered along, the fog finally lifted, and the sun began to shine. I quickened my steps and turned the corner of Pelham Road. There I saw my friend, Diana Hobbs, playing out in the street with one of her twin brothers. They were whispering together, and as I drew level the boy came up to me and said,

"Your Mother's not dead, is she?" I looked at him oddly, "No, of course, she isn't." He turned back to Diana, "See," he whispered, and I heard Diana whisper again, "She is."

I turned away and carried on until I reached our gate. I walked up the path feeling scared and knocked on the door. My brother Brian opened it, and he looked as if he had been crying. The feeling of foreboding deepened as I went into the front room, and I was surprised to see Daddy at home sitting in his chair by the window. The curtains were drawn shut. He held out his arms and took me onto his lap, looking very solemn.

"What's happened?" I whispered, "How is Mummy?" I added with a sick feeling in the pit of my stomach.

"Well," he began, "the doctor came, and she won't be getting better." "Oh. I know that she will!" I cried, convinced he was wrong. "No," Daddy replied, and then with a pause, "she's gone!" With that, tears began to fall down his face.

I had never seen my father cry; it was the most awful experience seeing him like that. By now we were both crying together while I clung onto his neck. I felt numb.

There was a gentle tap at the door; my father gently removed my arms from around his neck as Brian came in and announced, "They are here."

My father turned to me, "Stay here, and don't touch the curtains," he said, wiping his eyes, as he left the room.

I curled up on the chair and continued to weep. I didn't realize that the undertakers had arrived to take my Mother away. I didn't see her before she went, and I never saw her again. I was twelve years old, Brian fifteen, David was nine and Christopher only six.

The next few days went by in a haze. I can remember having strange dreams. Once I dreamt that I saw Mummy at the foot of my bed, but she was young and slim and was wearing a floral dress that Thelma had made for her. I awoke, but she wasn't there.

On the day of my Mother's funeral, David, Christopher and I were sent to Mrs. Clayton's. It was considered better for us not to go to the funeral. Elsie Clayton decided to take us to Danson Park to 'take our minds off things.'

Christopher, being only six years old, was not told about Mummy dying. Sheila, instead, said to him that she was in the hospital. Later, when he was seven and kept asking when she was coming back, he was told she had gone to heaven to live with the Angels. Then he came to find me.

"Did you know Mummy has gone to live with the Angels," he asked. I nodded.

"I didn't know that," he said thoughtfully and wandered off deep in thought.

I don't remember much about us going to the park with Mrs. Clayton, except that we sat by the lake and had a picnic. Still, I can remember returning to the house and finding it bursting at the seams with relations I didn't know. One of my cousins, Rona, (Auntie Lily's daughter), was there with her husband Stanley. It was the first time I had met her. She asked my father if she could take me to stay with her and Stanley and their two children Jane and Richard, for a few days. My father agreed, he thought it would take my mind off things. He had to try and work out how he was going to look after his large family, and so when my cousin and her family left, they took me along with them.

I felt numb and awkward and shy of these people I didn't know, as we travelled towards London in their car. We arrived at their home in Peckham Rye, South London.

My cousins lived in a flat over a flower shop, which Rhona and Stanley owned and ran together. When Rhona showed me around the shop, I was in heaven. Being surrounded by flowers, to me, was amazing, and I wanted to stay and help her with them. However, my cousin thought it best if I went with Jane to the park. (She probably wanted us out of the way).

Jane was nine and very smart for her age. She took me out in a rowing boat on the lake and taught me how to row. I was so happy that I could manage to row the boat, and we spent the afternoon taking turns rowing around the lake together.

I stayed for a week with my cousins, but by the end of the week, I wanted to go home to things more familiar as I was missing Mummy, my family and Daddy. On arriving back, Sheila gave me a big hug. "We have missed you," she said.

Incidentally, Rhona wrote many books on the art of floristry and flower arranging. Years later, she and Stanley were to start a

School for Floristry in The Old School House in Gloucestershire in southwest England. It was called "Flower Design of Great Britain," and Stanley became president of an international floral delivery service called Interflora.

When I returned home, I realized that I had caught the floristry 'bug' and that my interest in 'all things that grew' would stay with me for the rest of my life.

By now, it was time to return to school. We had exams before the Easter holidays. Now, we would see which girls would be going on to the Technical School and which girls would be continuing at the Central School.

It seemed strange going back to school after all that had happened, and I found it difficult to concentrate and take it all in.

My classroom was on the second floor of the school overlooking the cemetery where Mummy was buried. I had walked past this place so many times on my way to school with my mother. Now I would sit and gaze out of the school window and wonder how Mummy felt, lying there. It was so hard to concentrate on the lessons with my mind continually wandering.

Thelma had told me that when she was looking after Mummy on that awful day and waiting for the doctor to visit, that she had looked in on her. As Mummy seemed cold Thelma had given her a hot water bottle to warm her, not realizing that she was already dead. Then the doctor arrived and broke the news to her.

We had waited for three days for the doctor to find time to visit Mummy. Too bad, he left it too late to save her. As he didn't know the cause of death, there was to be a post-mortem. We discovered that she had died of double-pneumonia and pleurisy.

11

THE END OF AN ERA

We were all growing up, and Brian and I had to make frequent trips to the doctor for his asthma medication. We were seeing a different Doctor, as Daddy didn't want to deal with the old one. He couldn't help but think that our former doctor might have saved Mummy if he had come sooner to see her.

Our new Doctor thought it would be a good idea if Brian and I were to have an allergy test to find out what was triggering our asthma. So we were sent to Shooters Hill Hospital. Brian and I were both shown in the room where we were to have the tests. "Who is going to be first?" asked the nurse, waving a syringe.

Brian pointed to me, "She can go first." He said anxiously, not liking the look of this. I rolled up my sleeve, revealing the inside of my arm. As I was given the ten allergy injections up my arm, five each side, Brian passed out on the floor.

I suppose it was not a good idea for him to stand and watch. When he had recovered, he had to endure what I did. It transpired that I was allergic to house dust and duck feathers. It appeared that I did not react with the pollens, for that, I was happy. Now we were to stop taking the Ephedrine Hydrochloride tablets. Instead, we were to use the Rybar Inhaler. This was a plastic contraption consisting of a face mask with an attached container of medication, and a rubber bulb, which was squeezed to administer the medicine, while at the same time breathing in deeply.

The one thing I didn't like about it was that if I was to lick my lips after using it, they tasted like earwax. *(Not that I am in the habit of eating earwax, you understand.)* But the inhaler worked very well, and even better, instantly. Thank goodness, no more imagining that my head, hands and feet were growing larger by the minute, as the did when I took the Ephedrine tablets!

At school, it was time for the results of the exam, and find out who had been successful in moving to the Technical School and who would stay. I hoped that I could move on.

Most of the girls had their results already, and my teacher asked me if I had mine. I replied that I hadn't, and so I assumed that I would be staying there.

When I got to school on Monday, I was told to go and see the Headmistress, Miss Britain. She handed me a letter. It said that I had passed the exam. I was amazed and happy that I would be following in Sheila and Thelma's footsteps to Bexley Technical School.

Even though I was thrilled, I thought that they had made a mistake. I couldn't possibly have passed the exams. I assumed that they had felt sorry for me as I had lost my Mother and so decided to cheer me up!

Sheila was delighted when I got home and told her the news. She had left her job now, where she had been looking after the greyhounds at Crayford Stadium. She was at home all the time now to look after Daddy and us, and though I missed my mother dreadfully, it was lovely having Sheila to look after us.

"Oh, well done!" Sheila exclaimed when I showed her the letter from Miss Britain. "You are going to love it there," she added.

Daddy was just as delighted when he returned from his work in Leicester Square. He was now working for British Insulated Calenders Cables Construction Limited as an assistant secretary. Wearing the black homburg hat, he now wore, grieving every day for my Mother, he wore that hat until the day he died.

"It's good to have some good news for a change," he said, smiling at me and hugging me. I returned his smile, feeling glad that we had something to smile about.

I told Sheila that we were having an end of term concert and that I had been asked, along with the rest of the girls in my class, to help with the catering. We were to bring some cakes to school and hand them out to the parents. Sheila disappeared upstairs for a moment and came back down, carrying a pretty pink taffeta apron. It had a green frill around it and a green pocket. She handed it to me saying,

"You can wear this. I made it when I was at school in the needlework class."

I took the apron and tried it on; it was beautiful. I felt very grand and gave a twirl.

Although I missed my Mother, it seemed that everyone was extra kind. Even my brothers were nice to me! Of course, all my friends knew about my mother.

On the evening of the concert, I found myself the centre of attention – something I hadn't experienced at school before and it felt good. As I went around, offering cakes and being attentive to everyone's needs, one of the girl's fathers remarked what a brave girl I was and that I was an excellent example to the other girls. On the contrary, I felt guilty at feeling so happy with the pretty apron and all the attention I was getting.

Once again it was time to go shopping for a new school uniform, only this time I was with Sheila, and we were now shopping for a grey skirt, blazer and cardigan, white blouses, together with a grey beret and a maroon and grey striped tie. I was also going to have a P.E. kit, which consisted of grey skirt-like shorts and blue short-sleeved Airtex blouses. I was looking forward to not having to wear that horrid brown gymslip

I was to spend the first year in an annex of the Technical School. It was in an old Manor House in the country, in a place called Wilmington, which was not very far from Dartford. I would have to catch a green double-decker bus, the 401, every day from outside the Palace Cinema in Chapel Road, which was right opposite the Congregational Church.

Two double-decker buses stopped there. One was for the girls and one for the boys whose school was on the other side of our School woods.

I loved my new school. It reminded me of the boarding schools I had read about in the Girl's Crystal comics that my friend Rosina had given me. I had spent days lying on my bed reading through all the school stories contained in these comics.

At Wilmington Manor, there was a beautiful rose walk and sunken garden, a summerhouse and vast woods where we could wander among the trees and listen to the song of the birds. We would stand on a wooded hill overlooking the valley where the boys' school was, and spend the whole of the lunch break waving to the boys, and giggle as they waved back. For some reason, they seemed more interesting to me now that I was growing older!

I loved this school. The classrooms all had beautiful rooms with ornate high ceilings and imposing windows. There was a lily pond in the sunken garden and bench seats. I made friends with a girl called Barbara Smith. She wore her long blonde hair in two thick braids, and she had a large brown mole on each cheek, which fascinated me.

One Thursday, the last two lessons being Art, our Art Mistress allowed the two of us to take our charcoal and paper and go and sit in the summerhouse at the end of the rose-walk, to sketch.

Barbara and I chattered and laughed together as we sketched, so didn't hear the final bell. Meanwhile, our teacher had forgotten that she had permitted us to draw outside. When we finally returned to our classroom, everyone had left to go home, and we had missed the girls' school bus. So we had to wait for the next one, which just happened to be the boys' bus! Hm.

With red faces, we climbed on amidst much catcalling and whistles. You would think they had never seen a girl before!

But we thoroughly enjoyed the attention we received. I think it was about this time that I discovered I was quite fascinated by boys. Funny, seeing as I had three brothers, but somehow these boys were different and much more interesting to me than Brian, David and Christopher were.

One of the highlights of our time at this school was being bussed to a nearby college to use their swimming pool and have swimming lessons. Our teacher was very concerned that I might get cold and trigger an attack of asthma. So, she always pulled me out after I had spent about ten minutes in the water, so I never really had time to learn to swim!

We had a girl called Diane in our class who loved to show off. One day, while we were in the changing room, she decided to demonstrate her diving skills, so she dived off the bench and unintentionally, went straight through a window. She ended up with a substantial jagged cut on her arm, where she had put it through the window as she jumped off the bench. We were appalled at the amount of blood she lost. Fortunately, first aid was at hand, and so Diane was rushed to a hospital.

Because of her "stupidity," our swimming lessons were suspended for a while, to instill in us the childishness of fooling around in the changing rooms.

That summer, we staged an outdoor play on the stretch of lawn behind the Manor house. It was "Hiawatha", and the setting was perfect for it, with the woods as a backdrop. We invited the inmates of a local nursing home to watch it. The whole thing was a great success, and they thoroughly enjoyed it, even shouting "Bravo!" at the end.

I loved the time I spent at Wilmington Manor. I didn't ever want to leave it, and that was the feeling for all the girls there.

On February 6th, 1952, we were all made to assemble in the hall. The Headmistress, Miss Pike, looked very serious.

"Good afternoon, ladies," she began. I loved the way we were referred to as "Ladies" at this school; it made me feel so grown up.

Miss Pike continued, “I have some very sad news to impart. You will remember this day for the rest of your lives,” she declared and went on.“Our much beloved King, King George 6th, has passed away, which means that we now have a Queen.

His eldest daughter Princess Elizabeth is now our Queen. She will be known as Queen Elizabeth the second and her husband, Prince Philip Mountbatten shall be known as the Duke of Edinburgh.”

There was a shocked silence, and then we were all told to go back to our classes.

Some girls began to cry; others whispered amongst themselves. Once the lessons were finished for the day, we sat around in groups discussing this news until it was time to catch the bus home.

“What would it be like to have a Queen,” we wondered.

That feeling of uncertainty came over me again. That familiar feeling I felt when Mummy died. Why did nothing ever stay the same? I felt so sad and strange.

In the days following, the Newspapers, with black borders, showed endless pictures of the remaining Royal family in black and heavily veiled faces, their faces almost unrecognizable beneath. There were the last pictures of the King, waving goodbye to Princess Elizabeth and Prince Philip as they went on a tour of Africa. Then there were pictures of a very pale Princess Elizabeth returning early from her trip.

The last photos of the King showed him hatless, there was a cold wind blowing, and everyone said he must have caught a cold without his hat. It was announced later that he had died of cancer.

The funeral of the King was a very sombre affair. We had all loved him for the concern he had shown for his subjects during the war. He had refused to leave London during the Blitz even though Buckingham Palace was also bombed. We all adored the Queen whom, we were informed, would now be known as Queen Elizabeth the Queen Mother. It was so sad to see the Queen Mother and her two daughters all shrouded in thick black veils.

We were told this would now be the new 'Elizabethan Age" and that things would continue to get better. "Well, thank goodness for that!" We thought.

After the King's lying in state in Westminster Abbey and his well deserved, elaborate state funeral, his eldest daughter Elizabeth would be crowned Queen in Westminster Abbey.

History was happening before our eyes when a friend of my sister Sheila asked us if we would like to go and see the Coronation on her new Television. At that time, there were not many people who owned a television; we included, so we were not surprised to see the room full of strangers when we got there.

I remember we sat all day and watched while Sheila's friend fed us tinned salmon and tomato sandwiches smothered in lots of salt and pepper. It was the first time I had tasted salmon and tomato sandwiches, and I remember finding them so delicious.

How wonderful it was, to see the golden carriage, even though we were viewing it in black and white. (Later we were able to see the colour supplements in the Newspapers.) How beautiful Princess Elizabeth looked in her creamy satin and gold, richly embroidered dress, with a fabulous long train held by all her ladies in waiting.

When she sat on the throne wearing her weighty bejewelled crown and carrying the orb and mitre, she looked every inch a

Queen. Even though at 23 years, she still seemed so young. It was also lovely to see little Prince Charles and his sister Princess Anne, standing by their Grandmother watching their mother crowned Queen. We all felt proud to have her as our Queen, and we were convinced our lives would now be much better as we were entering a new 'Elizabethan age.'

Now there was the Festival of Britain to look forward to in London with the new strange-looking buildings, which included the thin cigar-shaped Skylon and the seemingly, enormous new Festival Hall.

Thelma went to see the sights with her friends from Liberty's. She returned and told us all about it.

"It was just amazing," she said, her eyes shining. "I have never seen anything like the Skylon before. We had such a wonderful time."

12

ANOTHER WEDDING

MY YEAR AT WILMINGTON HAD NOW COME TO AN END. SHEILA was still home, looking after the family. Daddy was still working in Leicester Square, he had terrible Osteoarthritis in both hips and now walked with a cane. He would hook the cane to his bike while he rode to and from the station every day to catch the train.

"My leg's giving me Gyp," he would say as he walked painfully.

Daddy did try and have some physiotherapy for his hip but would return home from these sessions in even more pain, so he gave up going. He found it increasingly difficult to get around. Still, he stayed wonderfully cheerful and was always telling jokes and pulling faces to make us laugh. Dear Daddy.

He had given up his allotment but still produced beautiful vegetables in our garden. He provided our family with lots of runner beans, cabbage and tomatoes. I know his hip was bothering him as he used to spend a lot of time sitting on the kitchen stool in the garden, smoking his pipe.

He would engage in conversation with Mr. Mepham next door, or Harry and Jack Curtis, the two brothers who lived on the other side of us. They had lived there with their mother, who was a sweet little old lady. When I was about six years old, she presented me with a beautiful paper sunshade and a fan.

Betty was happily married to Robert. By now, they had a second child, a daughter Helen, as well as Robert junior. Thelma was still working at Liberty's in Regent Street as a seamstress. She learned how to make clothes for the rich and famous. She would bring home the most amazing scraps of material, brocades, satins, and sequin-covered tulle that I would use to make dresses for my dolls. I had the best-dressed dolls in the whole of Bexleyheath!

One day, Ronald Jackson, who lived along the road, started to 'call on' Sheila. He was tall with dark hair and piercing blue eyes. He was smitten and would bring his guitar and serenade her.

One of his favourite songs was 'Oh My Darling Clementine.'

Sitting on a chair in our living room, he strummed his guitar and sang:

> *"Oh my darling, oh my darling, oh my darling,*
> *Clementine.*
> *You are lost and gone forever, dreadful sorry,*
> *Clementine."*

and ending with,

> *"How I missed her, how I missed her, how I missed*
> *my Clementine.*
> *But I kissed her little sister (looking at me) and*
> *forgot my Clementine."*

"Hm." I thought. He is not kissing me!

Ron laughed at the expression on my face. He was teasing me, of course.

Within the year, Sheila and Ron were married at our Congregational Church in Chapel Road. As money was still very scarce, it wasn't a very grand affair. They married on a cold and frosty February 14th, Valentine's Day, which was also Ron's birthday.

Sheila wore a dark green suit, as green was her favourite colour, and carried a matching green muff decorated with a spray of mixed freesias. On her head was a green, head-hugging hat.

Thelma was 'Chief Bridesmaid' and wore a grey suit. She carried a matching muff, also with freesias adorning it. Her hat was similar to Sheila's, but it was grey.

I was designated as being a bridesmaid and wore a navy wool coat, which was not new. I did get a new navy head-hugging felt hat to wear, and a corsage for my lapel.

Ron had a found job in Scotland as a teacher, so once more, we were saying goodbye. This time to Sheila, our second mother and, of course, to the happy couple as they left to begin their new life. This time though, this 'goodbye' was a joyous occasion. Sheila and Ron were to live in a newly built house in East Kilbride, Lanarkshire. "You must come and visit once we're settled," Sheila told us, seeing our sad faces.

So, now it was Thelma's turn to look after us. Thelma had given up her job at Liberty's, as she couldn't manage to do both. She was twenty now and took the role of the mother very seriously. I am afraid she didn't get much help from me. Both David and

Christopher were typical teenage boys and were always getting into scrapes. Brian, of course, was usually out with his friends.

Daddy was pleased to have Thelma's help with the washing, cleaning and cooking. On her twenty-first birthday, he bought her an ironing board, as we didn't have one, thinking it would make her life more comfortable. I thought it was a strange gift, and I know Thelma was disappointed, but she never said anything.

It must have been hard for her to take us all on, at her young age. Now, I wish I had helped her more, but being a selfish teen, I never saw the need.

One day Brian was making a model airplane, and David picked up the small tube of cement, put it in his mouth and promptly swallowed it! At eleven years old, you would think he would know better!

"I think you had better go to casualty and have it checked out," Thelma said, looking worried.

"Don't worry," I said, "I'll take him up to Shooters Hill Hospital."

On recollection, it would have been quicker to take him to the Cottage Hospital where they took me when I was knocked down by the car. But having been to Shooters Hill Hospital with Brian recently, it was the first thing that came into my head.

By now, it was about teatime, but David and I went to catch the bus to Welling Corner. We waited for fifteen minutes before the bus arrived, then boarded another bus for the emergency department at Shooters Hill Hospital. We waited for ages to see the doctor, who finally told me, "Not to worry; it would pass out the other end in due course!"

We were relieved, but it was now dark, and about eleven o'clock in the evening, and so the buses had stopped running. David and I had mistakenly thought the hospital staff would arrange for us to ride in an ambulance back to our home. That, we discovered, was not going to be possible. So, we started to walk home. There was no other alternative.

We had begun walking down Shooter's hill towards Welling when David announced, "I'm not walking all that way!" He promptly raised his thumb at a passing lorry, which slowed down and pulled over, a little way ahead of us. As we approached it, the driver peered down at us from high in his cab. "Where are you going?" He asked us. "To Bexleyheath clock tower," I replied "Hop in then," he said, grinning, "I happen to be going past there."

David and I clambered up into the cab beside him. "What a new, exciting experience!" I thought to myself. "Imagine us; riding in a lorry! It's so high up!"

As the lorry driver drove off with David and me, he asked, "What are you two doing out at this hour?"

I explained what had happened, about my brother eating glue. The driver saw the funny side, and we all had a good chuckle. "Thank goodness he had come along at that moment." I thought. "It would have taken us all night to walk home otherwise."

David did recover from the experience, and also he learned a valuable lesson, "Keep things out of my mouth!"

13

SCHOOL LIFE

After finishing the school year at Wilmington, I was transferred to the leading Bexley Technical School in Townley Road, Bexleyheath. I would be walking to school now, instead of catching the bus.

I got back into my schoolwork at 'Bexley Tech' and was actually beginning to enjoy the lessons! The school had a massive field with tennis courts, a hockey pitch, and a netball pitch in the playground. On the days when we had games and gym, we were to take a shower afterwards. How I hated that! The school provided the towels, which were not much bigger than a tea towel, and had holes in them. These tiny towels left nothing to the imagination!

I was very embarrassed to undress in front of the other girls. I was still quite small for my age and very self-conscious of my skinny body. In contrast, the other girls were all becoming young ladies, and their developing chests were quite apparent. Many times I would find excuses not to have a shower. One such explanation was, "I'm not feeling well enough to take part in Gym or games, because of my asthma." When I'd used that one, I was told to sit outside the Head Mistress's study and read a book.

In actual fact, my asthma attacks prevented me from running. So, when we were playing hockey, I was the person to be put in goal and given the large leg pads to wear. I think both the team and the teacher gave up on me ever becoming any good. When, standing in the goalmouth, wearing the large hockey pads, I would jump over the hard hockey ball – just in case it hit me!

In the summertime, we would play tennis in the school tennis courts. One day my friend Barbara and I were enjoying our game, even though I didn't hit the ball very often. We were having so much fun that when the bell rang for the next lesson, we continued to play.

We had ignored the fact that everyone was going to the showers to wash and clean up before going to the next class, and somehow this didn't seem to bother us at all.

The repercussion of our decision is that we were going to be late for music class if we needed to shower. So we skipped having our shower and made our way to the next lesson, arriving fifteen minutes late!

After class, our music teacher reprimanded us severely and promptly sent us to the Head Mistress.

Miss Collins, the headmistress, said that she wouldn't put up with our "tardiness and disrespect." She ranted and raved at us and then she pointed her finger at me. "Why are you wearing coloured ribbons in your hair?" She yelled angrily, her face turning red. "Your Mother knows they are supposed to be white!"

I burst into tears. Miss Collins, still fuming, dismissed us and told us, "Do not be late ever again for any lesson!"

I was still sobbing when we reached the needlework lesson. Miss Cowie, our needlework teacher, asked me why I was crying. Barbara told her."Miss Collins told Wendy that her mother shouldn't make her wear coloured ribbons in her hair, but her mother is dead!"

Miss Cowie promptly left the classroom with a purposeful expression. When she returned, Miss Cowie told me that Miss Collins would want to see me after the needlework lesson.

I was dreading coming face to face with her again, but when I went to see the Headmistress, she smiled at me kindly. She said she was sorry, and that she didn't know about my mother.

After that, whenever she saw me in the corridor, she would single me out and chat a little with me. Miss Collins went out of her way to make sure I was alright, and I felt much better after that. She was very kind to me.

I suppose one can't be good at everything, though the two things I did excel in were English and Art. I loved both of these subjects. I also enjoyed acting in our school plays. I can remember a play we performed about a northern mining town. With memories of our evacuation to Padiham still reasonably fresh in my mind, I was able to recite a perfect Lancashire accent! The teacher was very impressed and told the class that it wasn't the last they would hear of me. What a shame that never came true.

I enjoyed the art lessons. My painted portrait of 'a tramp' hung in the Tate Art Gallery in London's Trafalgar Square as part of a School's exhibition of art. Sadly though, that talent never went anywhere either.

I enjoyed the assemblies we had each morning. Our headmistress would sit on the platform. She would smile as our voices rose singing the hymns. Whenever a particular rendition especially pleased her, Miss Collins would make us sing it, again and again.

She was an excellent Head Mistress and was very proud of her girls' achievements. She was always remarking about how this company, and that company, were requesting a 'gel' from Bexley Tech.

While in assembly, we were to sit on our chairs with our knees together, and both feet on the floor. Our hands were to be in our laps when we weren't holding the hymn books. "Woe betide any girl who moved," Miss Collin's warned. Her eagle eye would spot that girl, and she would point and shout,

"That girl there is moving. Come and see me later!"

The feet on the floor, hands in the lap habit has never left me. To this day, I find myself sitting this way, especially in Church.

The rules in school were stringent. We walked in single file along the corridors of the school. If a teacher approached, we had to stand to one side in respect until she had passed. Then we could continue on our way. It certainly taught us respect. I, for one, wouldn't dream of disobeying a rule once it was learned.

Miss Collins was awarded the 'Order of the British Empire' for her services as a Head Mistress. On the day after she received the award, we were all gathered in the hall for assembly.

The teachers, seated in their places on the stage, around a small, higher platform which held the Head's table and chair.

We sang the hymn, and when we sat down, the headteacher told us about the award and how our Head Mistress had gone to Buckingham Palace to receive it from the Queen.

Miss Collins wearing her award, beamed proudly at us and related the story of her visit to the Palace, before sitting back down. Unfortunately, the back legs of her chair slipped off the back of the platform.

Miss Collins went over backwards and treated us all to a full view of her legs and feet sticking up in the air, before disappearing behind the table. There was a deathly hush while we all waited with bated breath to see what would happen next. You could have heard a pin drop.

Just then, her slightly pink, smiling face appeared above the tabletop. As she climbed to her feet, she pronounced, "Remember girls," she said, "Pride comes before a fall! Let that be a lesson to you!"

Relieved that she was unhurt, we all fell about laughing. That was a sight we would not forget for a long, long time! It was the subject of many a discussion in the classrooms later.

Another class I enjoyed was 'Domestic Science and House Wifery.' In this class, we would learn how to cook, how to do laundry, and how to 'keep' a house. Our Headmistress lived in an apartment at the school. We had to take it in turns to clean for her and cook her meals.

It was all useful training for us, and we enjoyed it. We brought items of clothing to school and were taught how to wash them by hand, shown the correct way to iron clothes, fold linen, and even how to treat iron mould stains with the juice of a lemon.

We had to starch any table linens but not with a spray because they didn't exist, but by mixing the starch powder with water and adding it to the rinse. The linens would emerge, quite stiff from the wash, and it would iron beautifully. If we were washing white garments, we would add a little blue bag to the water, which contained a hard, blue, reusable substance, wrapped in muslin and tied with a string. Wc would lower it into the water, still holding the length of string, until the water had turned dark blue. Then we would take it out again. The blue tint made the whites shine.

Our teacher taught us how to iron linen 'on the right side first' to give it a shine. Then turn it over and iron the other side, so that any embroidery would stand out better.

I learned the correct way to iron a shirt. First, the collar, then the cuffs and sleeves and lastly, the body. Finishing with the perfect way to fold the garment. Daddy was thrilled to receive his shirts so well laundered.

When we baked, we had to wash the saucepans and dishes by hand, and they were given an inspection afterwards. Anything that wasn't spotless had to be re-washed. Miss Mason would test the cleanliness of the pots and pans by running her hand around inside them. We were to scrub the wooden tables where we had worked with a bar of Sunlight soap and a scrubbing brush!

Back then, some of the lesson subjects were quite different from those taught in the school curriculum today. We studied these subjects: English, English Literature, French, Spanish, German, Arithmetic, Mental Arithmetic, Geometry, Algebra, Science, Domestic Science, House Wifery, Music, Art, Gym, Games, Dancing, Religious Instruction, History, Geography, Needlework and Embroidery.

We were also taught Verse Speaking, the correct way to speak the Queen's English. We had to recite:

"My Dame has a lame tame crane
My Dame has a crane, which is lame
Pray gentle Jane, let my Dame's lame, tame crane
Feed and come home again."

The words with 'a' in them had to be accentuated as in "la-eem, ta-eem, cra-een." Then, we had to say out loud, "Ppppppppppppp," and "Bbbbbbbbbb." We learned poems like 'Meg Merrilees' by John Keats.

"Old Meg she was a Gipsy
And liv'd upon the Moors;
Her bed it was the brown heath turf,
And her house was out of doors."

And 'The Flower Seller.' by Eleanor Farjeon.

"The Flower-seller's fat, and she wears a big shawl!
She sits on the curb with her basket and all;
The wares that she sells us are not very dear
And are always the loveliest things of the year.
Daffodils in April,
Purple flags in May,
Sweet peas like butterflies
Upon a summer day,
Brown leaves in autumn,
Green leaves in spring,
And berries in the winter
When the carol-singers sing.
The Flower-seller sits with her hands in her lap,
When she's not crying Roses, she's taking a nap;
Her bonnet is queer, and she calls you My dear,

And sells you the loveliest things of the year."

We took embroidery lessons with our form mistress, Miss Cowie, who also taught us how to use a treadle sewing machine. I learned how to sew smocking and Italian quilting. I once fashioned a smocked baby's dress using soft woollen Vyella material. I sewed a satin cushion using Italian quilting. I joined cotton backing to the 'wrong side' of the satin, then stitched a double line pattern by hand using tiny running stitches, creating channels. A cotton cord was threaded through the channels to create the design.

No matter how skilled I was in these crafts, I remained hopeless at maths. Generally, I found Algebra and Geometry a little easier. I used to have nightmares about being asked for the answers in the Mental Arithmetic class. Then I came up with an idea! When the teacher would ask a math question, I would put my hand halfway up. It was very likely that she wouldn't want me to share the answer! Happily, for me, it worked!

As we were to walk to different classrooms for different lessons, I hated going to the Geography class. The Geography room smelled of stale air. The teacher had a medical condition that meant she was always cold. She refused to open any windows and would wear a coat as she sat at her desk. If any girl talked in her class, they were to stand on their chair for the entire lesson. We found this gruelling, especially as the air closer to the ceiling was hot and fetid.

Our Geography teacher was one of the most unpopular teachers, and I don't think we learned much about Geography from her, either.

The girls who were to become nurses were given extra science lessons, and those who were training to be secretaries or working in offices learned typing and shorthand.

One day in the Domestic Science class, while sitting at the tables waiting for the teacher to arrive, we could smell gas. My friend, Barbara, claimed that she knew a way to find a leak. So, she lit a match and went looking for it.

As you might expect, there was a loud bang as the gas ignited. Luckily all Barbara suffered with was singed hair and disappearing eyebrows!

We were given a sharp talking to and learned that looking for a gas leak with a naked flame was not a wise idea!

In dancing class, we learned ballroom dancing. For some reason unknown to me, I was always chosen to play the man!

We also learned ballet. The teacher invited the parents to our ballet performance of 'The Magic Flute,' an opera written by Wolfgang Amadeus Mozart. I played the part of Monostatos, the black moor. I loved to dance, and the performance was a great success.

Afterwards, one of the teachers asked if I was part of 'Ballets Russes,' a ballet company founded in Paris in 1909 by the Russian impresario Serge Diaghilev. The original company included the choreographer Michel Fokine and the dancers, Anna Pavlova and Vaslav Nijinsky. She thought she had seen me dancing with them at Covent Garden. I told her it wasn't me, but I wished it was. I felt very flattered by her comment, even though I am quite sure my dancing was not as good as the dancer she had seen.

During my time at this school, because I was still very tiny, I was directed to play a six-year-old in the next school play. My small size was due to asthma that I suffered. We believed that it had stopped me from growing. Well, that plus the shortage of food during the war. Thankfully, the following year, when I turned fifteen, I suddenly shot up and became tall and willowy instead of short and skinny.

Every year we were to study one of William Shakespeare's plays. Our drama teacher chose to perform "Twelfth Night," and she cast me as Lady Olivia. I was to wear a long black taffeta dress, a Spanish veil, called a 'mantilla' in my hair and was to carry a big black fan. I was very keen to play this part, so I diligently learned the words. I can still remember them:

"Make me a willow cabin at your gate.
And call upon my soul within the house.
Write loyal cantons of contemned love
And sing them loud even in the dead of night.
Halloo your name to the reverberate hills.
And make the babbling gossip of the air.
Cry out, "Olivia!"
Oh, you should not rest
Between the elements of air and earth
But you should pity me."

Unhappily, echoing my fate long ago when I missed the chance of being the bluebell fairy, I fell sick on the day and was unable to take part. My understudy hadn't bothered to learn the words and, I was told afterwards, went on stage with the book tucked behind her fan. Unfortunately, she forgot she was hiding the book and turned her back on the audience. Her secret had been revealed, they all saw that she was reading her lines. She and the rest of the class were mortified, but the audience thought it was hilarious.

Thelma and I attended the Congregational Church occasionally, and I eventually became a Sunday school teacher teaching the five to seven-year-olds about Jesus. I loved to talk to the children and share bible stories with them, and it seems like every week, I was asked by a little five-year-old if he could marry me.

It was so lovely to hear the children sing:

"Down came the raindrops on a cloudy day,
Wetting all the pavements
Washing dirt away.
Waking little brown buds,
Thirsty seeds as well,
Right into the blades of grass
The tiny raindrops fell.
Pitter-patter raindrops
Listen how they came.
Pitter-patter raindrops
Let us do the same.
Pitter-patter raindrops
Children, though we be,
Giver of the welcome rain
We give our thanks to thee."

The children would use their hands to clap in time and move their arms as though washing the dirt away. One Sunday, they were singing this, and I was standing behind a table performing the actions with them. Unfortunately, I got carried away with the arm movements and knocked everything off the table!

I joined the Church Youth group called Pilots. We did our best to raise money to help the Missionaries. I can still remember the prayer we prayed at the end of each meeting.

> *"Teach us, Good Lord, to serve thee as*
> *thou deservest.*
> *To give and not to count the cost.*
> *To fight and not to heed the wound.*
> *To toil and not to seek for rest*
> *To labour and not to ask for any reward*
> *Save that of knowing that we do thy will."*

14

WORK AND OPERATIONS

I LEFT SCHOOL WHEN I WAS SIXTEEN. WELL, I WAS ALMOST seventeen as it was the summer of my seventeenth year. It felt strange walking out of school, knowing I would never be going back. But I felt quite elated at the thought. There were no graduation celebrations in those days.

I didn't have a clue as to what work I should do. Daddy suggested that I should work at Hides, the department store by the clock tower. So, he went to see the Manager and persuaded him to give me an interview. My father could be very persuasive when he put on his posh voice, and it was hard to say no to him. Daddy knew my difficulties with figures, so he told me, "Now, they will ask you what you are like at figures, so tell them that you are about average."

I sat in an office for my first job interview with Mr. Passmore, the managing director of Hides. He was a huge, intimidating man. I was shaking in my shoes. Sure enough, I was asked the question, "Now, how are you at Maths?" I replied as Daddy had instructed, and it worked! Mr. Passmore decided to hire me!

The store uniform consisted of a navy woollen skirt and white blouse. I thought we all looked very smart. I started by working in the wool department but was soon moved to the haberdashery, as a vacancy opened in that department. What a mistake that was!

Selling buttons from a card was not my idea of fun. The display buttons were attached to large pieces of cardboard, with the price displayed beneath each button. There was a card for each colour, and they were priced by the dozen. I had no idea how to work out the cost of five buttons at two shillings and eleven pence per dozen. There were no calculators in those days to help me out, and of course, the cash registers were not computerized. I would spend ages in the back storeroom trying to work it out, getting more and more worried while the customer got more and more annoyed at having to wait so long. Finally, Pam, my supervisor came to find me.

Taking pity on me, she showed me how to do it. "To find the price of one, divide the cost by twelve - for the dozen - and then multiply the answer by the number you need," she clearly explained.

My face brightened. "Oh, I see," I said, amazed at how easy it seemed. I wondered, was it really that easy, and why couldn't my teachers have told me that before? Although they probably had. No doubt, I had been daydreaming at the time!

How I had hated figures. All numbers were like a foreign language to me, which was not surprising, considering all the maths lessons I had missed at school.

Truthfully, I found working in the store a bit of a nightmare. It wasn't just the maths, the store cat recently had kittens. They were very playful. But, our counters were on legs, and as I walked back and forth behind the counter, they would jump out and cling to my ankles, digging their tiny claws into my leg. It made me a nervous wreck as I tried, without much luck, to dodge the flying furry creatures.

My favourite time was the morning break when we went upstairs to the canteen and had a coffee and a buttered currant bun. For lunch, I would go to the cake shop along the road and treat myself to a cream donut. It was amazing that I didn't add an ounce to the eight stone four pounds that I weighed. But I remained the same slender teen.

The canteen was the place to go on a Friday night, as they held a 'beetle drive' for the employees. A beetle Drive is when you sit at a table of 4 people each. Each player has a score sheet, and take it in turns to throw the dice.

You have to get a 6 first to draw a beetle's body; next, you must get a 5 to draw the head, 4 its wings, 3 a leg (you need 6 legs), 2 an antenna and 1 an eye. When someone has a completed beetle they shout "beetle," and the winner moves on to the next table ahead, while the one with the least parts drawn has to move to the table behind. Then we all start again.

On the other side of the Haberdashery department was the ribbon counter. They had a vast array of beautiful colourful ribbons. I found it was quite fascinating. The supervisor that ran the department was also named Pam. Her assistant was Sylvia Skeat. Sylvia was my age. She had a petite figure and was always neat and tidy (unlike me). We quickly became best friends when we discovered that we had something in common – we both suffered from asthma.

Sylvia and I would take our breaks together, and chat to the boys who came into the store to flirt with us. One day my supervisor handed me a note, given to her by a young man who lived in

Woolwich Road. The letter said that this young man would like to meet me and asked if I would accept his note "in lieu" of an introduction.

He wanted to take me to the cinema. I had never had a boyfriend and didn't know what to make of the offer, so I asked my supervisor, and she encouraged me to go. I didn't want my father to know, so I sent a note back, via my supervisor, saying I would meet him at his gate, and we could go from there.

So on the day arranged, I walked up Woolwich Road and met him at his gate. We said "Hello" and then proceeded to walk down the Broadway to the Regal Cinema. I felt so shy and couldn't think of anything to say to him. He must have felt the same because not a word passed between us until we got back to his gate after the film. Then he said, "Well, we didn't have much to say, did we?" I replied, "No, we didn't" then he asked me if I would like to go on another date with him. I replied, "I will think about it and let you know." I never saw him again, which, I suppose, is no surprise.

There was a department at Hides for alterations and for making drapes and curtains. A girl named Evelyn Perrot worked there. She had polio as a child, and so she wore a leg brace and walked with a limp. Evelyn was also anemic and would complain that her mother kept feeding her raw liver to try and help the condition. I must admit, her face was always pale, but with her flawless complexion and lovely natural golden hair, she was a beautiful girl.

Her best friend was Sybil Shove. Sybil worked in the wool department, where I had worked when I first started at Hides. When she was very young, she had had a heart condition, which had affected her growth. She was very tiny, less than five feet tall.

The four of us, together with another girl, Anne, became great friends and joined a youth club. It was held in a School in Barnhurst and was very popular with the young folk, now called 'teenagers.' Teenagers all imagined that we were being misunderstood and felt like James Dean in the film 'Rebel Without a Cause.'

It was a new experience for me to be mixing with boys and getting to know them. I had a crush on one boy called Derek Moore. I thought he was "just dreamy" with his dark hair and dark brown eyes. But he didn't seem to notice me. I was much too shy to approach him, even to the point of crossing to the other side of the road if I saw him coming.

Hiking with the youth club (Wendy in dark glasses)

One of our favourite things to do was to go hiking into the country. We went on some lovely walking trips with the youth club.

One time Thelma, Sylvia and I donned our new mode of dress, our jeans, and walked from Dartford to Eynsford across the fields. As we stopped to cool our hot and aching feet in the river, we were spotted by a photographer from the Daily Herald newspaper who took our picture for the paper!

Photograph in the Daily Herald newspaper

After hiking, we decided to go to sleep beside a haystack, until we were disturbed by something moving in the hay. It was full of mice! Boy, did we move!

When I was nineteen, my doctor decided it was time for me to have my bunions removed. I had bunions on both of my feet, making it very painful to walk. My big toes each had a medium-sized bunion. I was nineteen and had never had a boyfriend, and I was quite sure it was because of my ugly feet.

So, it was arranged. Dreading the operation, but looking forward to having straight feet, I went into the Southern Hospital just outside Dartford. This hospital, formerly a fever hospital, had been used for the T.B. epidemic that raged after the First World

War. It was way out in the country away from the town to minimize any spread of the disease.

The operation went without a hitch, although I came round while still in the operating theatre! After regaining consciousness, I could feel something going on with my feet, but without pain. The doctor noticed I had woken, put me back under the anesthetic and carried on. There were two different doctors, each working on a foot, so my left foot was made straighter than the right one!

It took me a few days to come round from the anesthetic because they had to give me a second dose. I can remember that I was crying a lot with the pain until a nurse told me to stop making such a fuss. Her words seemed to pull me out of my semi-conscious state, and I stopped crying and sat up to take in my surroundings.

I was in a large hospital ward with windows on three sides. There were a dozen beds, each with a locker beside it and a narrow, wheeled table stretching across the bed. A metal cradle lifted the covers off my feet and legs, now encased in Plaster-of-Paris from the tips of my toes right up to my knees.

In the bed next to me was a tiny and adorable, ninety-eight-year-old woman called Flo. Flo was blind, and she had broken her hip. On the other side of me was a middle-aged woman who had a similar operation to mine. Next to her was a woman who had broken her leg and had complications.

The nurses would come round and take our temperatures, waking us at six o'clock each morning. One Chinese nurse was always singing and had a beautiful voice. We so appreciated her cheerfulness.

A nurse put a thermometer into my mouth. "Lift your tongue. Have you had your bowels open?" She asked in the same breath. I tried to speak. "Don't talk while I take your temperature."

After they left and before the day-staff took over, the cleaning lady would come in with her floor polisher. The floors shone, and she was very proud of them. Sometimes she would stop by my bed for a chat. I noticed that she had lovely clear skin, and I asked her how she kept it so fresh.

"Oh," she replied, "I always use Nivea cream." Well, I thought, I must try that.

The days were very long in the hospital, having to be awake from 6 am. So I used to try and entertain the other patients with my antics.

One morning I hid at the bottom of my bed curled up under the cradle. When the nurse came in, she thought I had disappeared. She guessed something was up when the other patients started to laugh. I poked my head out and got a scolding, "You might think that's funny," she said, "but what if Matron had come around?" She said, crossly straightening my bedclothes.

I had forgotten about Matron. This woman was very strict and demanded that every bed be made correctly with envelope corners, and the bedspread "just so." Everyone was afraid of Matron in her dark blue dress and starched white cuffs and cap. Each bed was to be in line with the next one. No one was allowed to sit on top of the bedclothes. We all had to sit in the armchair by the bed throughout the day.

Matron would come around in the middle of the night and shine her torch in your eyes to see if you were still awake. I must admit she was very kind to me. Finding me awake, she would tell the nurse to get me some hot cocoa to help me sleep.

I stayed in the hospital for six weeks, during this time I had many visits from my friends. Sylvia, Evelyn, Sybil and Anne came to visit me. So did Thelma. Brian came with his friend, Donald. I felt very embarrassed, sitting up in bed in front of Donald. Brian bought me some wool to knit him a sweater. It was bright orange, and I hated the colour.

Because of the distance, I only got visited at weekends, so the weekdays would drag by. Brian sent me a funny letter, and so did Daddy:

Bexleyheath
20/2/55

My dear Puddenface,

I hope you are feeling better now, and that the pain is lessening. Do not let it get you down as the time will soon pass and you will be home again.

I will try to come and see you on Sunday if my leg is not too troublesome.

If I do not manage it I will try the following Sunday. I was thinking about you and hoping you will soon be home again so hurry up and get up on your hind legs.

Have you written to Sheila? Do write to her, I know she will soon reply.

I am afraid I have not much to write about so will close with love and best wishes.

Piepace

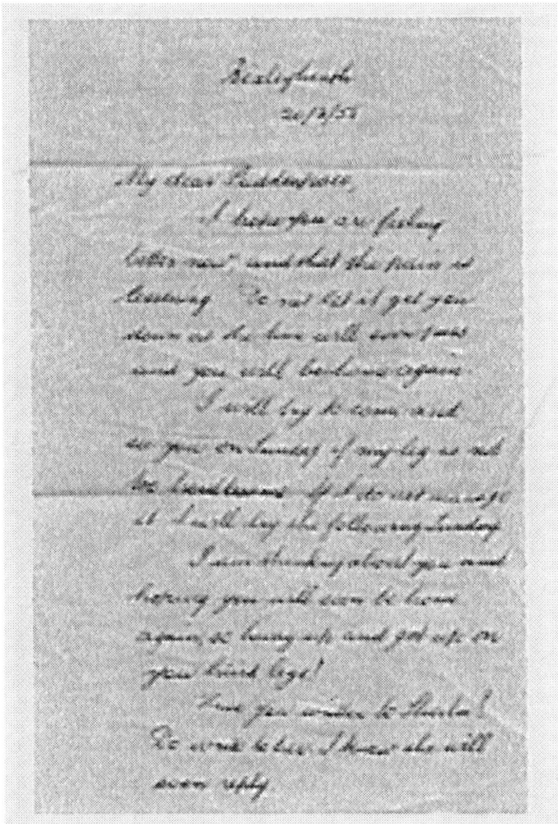

[illegible]
[illegible]

My dear [illegible],

I hope you are feeling better now and that the pain is lessening. Do not let it get you down as the time will soon pass and you will be home again.

I will try to come and see you on Sunday if my leg is not too troublesome. If I do not manage it I will try the following Sunday.

I am thinking about you and hoping you will soon be home again to hang up and get up on your hind legs!

Have you written to Sheila? Do write to her. I know she will soon reply.

I am afraid I have not much
to write about so will close with
love & best wishes

His penned illustration told me that my bicycle was waiting to be ridden and that Gyp was missing me. Daddy was suffering a lot with arthritis in his hips and found it challenging to get around. However, he did manage to pay me one visit, and I was so pleased to see him.

The nurses would give us blanket baths twice a week and washed our hair once every six weeks. The nurse had just washed my hair, and I was feeling so lovely and clean again. A 'ward orderly,' who was a little developmentally challenged, came by and poured orange juice over my head! The nurse didn't have time to rewash my hair, so I had to try and get the orange juice out with a wet flannel, it was so sticky, and I was very cross about it.

One of the older patients taught me how to crochet. I got on very well with it, churning out doilies so fast that a girl in the bed at the far end of the ward was impressed. She told me she would invite me to her wedding if I promised to make her a set of dinner mats. I said that I would, but I am ashamed to say I did not keep my promise, and when she invited me to her wedding, she was very disappointed that I had not done so.

Every day we had to sit in the chair beside the bed, with our feet up. I was so fed up with not being able to get up. So, I devised a way of getting around. By sitting on my narrow table on wheels and pushing off from the bed, I could propel myself around the ward from bed to bed. That was how I came to arrange Flo's pillows like an armchair and make her comfortable. Unfortunately, as she was blind, she was unaware of the time and would wake me in the middle of the night by calling, "Wendy, put my head right!" Of course, I obliged her.

The day finally came when it was time to have my plaster cast sawn off. What bliss to be free of that itchy stuff. The challenge of having to scratch an itchy leg by poking a knitting needle down beside the plaster was finally coming to an end.

I had a shock seeing my legs for the first time. After six weeks, they were as thin as the bones within them. As I hadn't been able to use my muscles, they had wasted somewhat. Also, I had forgotten how to walk. So, I was given electrical treatment each day to get the muscles working again. Wires from a machine were attached to my feet. My feet were then placed in a bowl of water while a charge was sent to the muscles in my feet and ankles, making them jump and making me jump as well! I looked at the scars on my feet. There were two, two-inch-long scars on each foot and of course, they were still painful to touch.

Spring was coming, and, by this time, I was longing to smell some fresh air. I kept asking the nurse if I could go outside. Finally, a nurse took me for a walk in the grounds. This young nurse held my arm, and we strolled around the hospital gardens. It was beautiful to see the bulbs coming up and listen to the birds singing. Unfortunately, the nurse slipped, and in trying to save herself from falling, she stepped on my foot.

“Oh, Wendy! I am so sorry!” She was so apologetic and sat me down on a bench to examine the damage. It transpired that in so doing, she had squeezed out a remaining stitch that had been missed by the doctor, so it was a blessing in disguise.

Finally, the day came when I was allowed to go home. It felt so good to be back with my family and to sleep in my own bed again. I couldn’t wait to go back to the youth club. I am not sure how we got to hear about it, but it was the place to go if you wanted to meet other teenagers. The club was very popular with all the teenagers in the area, and it was hosted by a formidable woman called Miss Tee. It was open every Monday to Friday and afforded somewhere for the youth of the surrounding area to hang out, rather than having to congregate on street corners and in shop doorways. Not that I ever did that, you understand!

At the club, we could dance as much as we wanted, and we would go on outings to the theatre or ice skating. After the operation, I could now wear the shoes that my friends were wearing, high heels and pointed toes. Dolcis, the shoe shop in the Broadway sold amazing shoes, mostly priced at forty-nine shillings and eleven pence. (Or 2 pounds nine shillings and eleven pence). That is about 2 pounds and 50p in today’s money. I would spend ages trying on shoes and deciding which ones to buy. I finally chose a pair of white court shoes with tiny stiletto heels. At last, I felt like my friends, and I wouldn't be (as I imagined) considered different! I told myself that it was alright to wear pointed toes, disregarding the fact that my toes were in the state they were before the operation *because* I had worn shoes that were too tight!

15

TEENAGERS

THESE YEARS WERE THE ERA OF ELVIS PRESLEY AND ROCK AND roll. We were teenagers and loving it. On Saturdays, we would all meet up at the Silver Lounge. The Silver Lounge was an ice-cream parlour in the Broadway past Christ Church. We could order a Knickerbocker Glory if we were hungry. It came in a very tall glass with fruit, nuts and ice cream, topped with a large swirl of cream, plus a long-handled spoon with which to eat it. I always found it challenging to finish as I was not used to consuming such a considerable amount of ice cream. Mostly though, we would have frothy coffee. Money didn't stretch very far. My pay of two pounds and ten shillings a week, minus the seventeen shillings and sixpence that I paid Thelma for my keep, meant that the money would be gone quickly. I would then flirt with the boys and chat about what we would do at the club or the dance hall that night.

At work, I was leaning on the counter as Sylvia came around the corner. "Coming to the club tonight?" she asked. "Yes," I replied, smiling. "What are you going to wear?"

"I'm not sure yet," Sylvia said, patting her perfect hair thoughtfully, "what are you wearing?"

"I think I shall wear my new pink skirt with my shell necklace and earrings," I replied, smiling in anticipation.

I had bought the shell necklace and earrings from the store with my first pay packet. They consisted of tiny snail shells painted all the colours of the rainbow. My second pay packet went on a beautiful necklace and earrings set, made up of pale blue glass flowers with pearl centres. My third week's pay went on a waist petticoat. It was pale blue nylon with blue guipure lace flowers around the hem and layers of tulle underneath. It made my skirts stand out, and when I danced, you could see the layers of tulle. As soon as I set eyes on it, I fell in love with it and had to have it.

After work, I got ready to go out. I dressed in a sleeveless pink pique blouse, with the collar turned up as fashion dictated. I put on my pink cotton circular skirt over my new petticoat, making it stand out. It made my 24-inch waist look even smaller!

After putting my long chestnut hair into a ponytail, I decided to don a pair of resin earrings shaped like very real pink cyclamen. I wore my new white high-heeled shoes and surveyed myself in the long mirror of our wardrobe. Pleased with the result, I pulled on my white cotton gloves, draped a white cardigan around my shoulders, grabbed my white plastic clutch bag, and ran downstairs.

Daddy was sitting in his armchair, listening to the radio. Thelma was in the kitchen ironing. She gazed wistfully at me, wishing she could come. Selfishly, it didn't occur to me that she wasn't happy to be staying at home doing the ironing with Daddy. I poked my head around the dining room door.

"Bye Dad. I'm off to the club."

My father looked up, "Right then, don't be late home."

"I won't," I replied over my shoulder as I ran out of the door.

I hurried down the road, my ponytail swinging to and fro. I was nineteen, and the world was my oyster!

I caught the bus to Marten's Grove and walked from there until I reached Woodside Road. It was a long road, and the club at the school was at the end. I eventually reached it and met up with the girls.

As we went in, the loud rock and roll music was playing in the hall. We all trooped into the girl's cloakroom to tidy our hair and fix our make-up.

In the room, the boys were grouped together at one end; some dressed as "Teddy boys," their hair combed into a quiff with long sideboards, wearing thin drainpipe trousers and thick-soled shoes. Meanwhile, the "Mods," with their impeccable short hair cuts, wore short-jacketed suits and Italian "winklepicker" shoes.

At the other end of the room, the girls were grouped too. Some, like me, were wearing their full skirts and flat or high-heeled shoes with pointed toes. Then there were the "mod" girls who wore tight-fitting dresses or skirts and huge beehive hairdos. Some of the points on their "winklepicker" shoes were so long, they appeared to turn up!

The groups each end of the room eyed each other, trying to attract the attention of a potential partner.

The next record to play was Elvis Presley's 'Jail House Rock.'

"Warden threw a party at the County jail….."

Sylvia grabbed my hand, and we started to jive. Our full skirts swung out as we turned, spinning. The boys turned and watched. Just then, two of them prised themselves from the group and came up to us. One took hold of Sylvia's hand, and the other grabbed mine. What a great feeling it was, dancing and swirling to the beat of the music. The tempo seemed to get faster and faster, and strangely, I found that I had the breath to do it!

The next record was a slow one, Pat Boone's 'April Love.' My partner was not into that, so he left me to walk myself back to the girls' end, watched by Evelyn, Sybil, and Anne.

The four of us decided to go and chat with Miss Tee, the club leader. She looked up from her paperwork as we entered her office. Her round, friendly face broke into a smile as she straightened her glasses.

"Hello," she beamed brightly, "and how are you?"

We chatted for a while, and then she told us that she was coming to make an announcement, so we went back into the club hall, followed by Miss Tee.

She signalled to the disc jockey to stop the music. When we were more or less all quiet, she held up her hand and said, "I have arranged for this year's summer holiday. In August, for two weeks, we will be going to Denmark! We shall be staying in a Danish farmhouse, and I need to know the numbers by the end of the month. There are thirty places available, and the money must be in as soon as possible."

Miss. Tee smiled as we all cheered. She turned and went to chat with the boys who had appeared from the snooker room, to repeat her message to them.

"Well," I said dejectedly to my friends, "There is no way that I could go."

Believing that I couldn't afford it, we chatted about the new holiday idea all evening. When I reached home, I told Daddy and Thelma about it. Daddy said, thoughtfully, "Maybe we could afford to let you go if you help with the cost."

"Oh, I would love to go too," Thelma said

"Well, couldn't you both go?" Daddy asked.

He didn't like the idea of me going on my own and was thinking that it would be a good idea for Thelma to go too so that she could keep an eye on me.

It transpired that Thelma and I were both able to go, with Daddy's help in paying some of the fares. We were so excited about it. We had never been abroad before.

So, Thelma and I began to make plans about what clothes we should take. Thelma had finished making me a beautiful deep turquoise-blue glazed cotton skirt with a four-inch deep waistband. I would wear it with my white short-sleeved blouse decorated with Guipure lace and of course I would have to take my pink skirt as well! We were going to have such a marvellous time together.

I had decided that I would like to have my hair cut. I was tired of my ponytail, but Daddy would not hear of it. So one day, Brian decided he could give me a new hairstyle, and so he got my brush and began to push my hair into another style. My hair ended up in a terrible tangle, with the brush caught up in it. I was furious at him. I went to Daddy.

"Look what Brian has done to my hair! I can't untangle it, how can I go out looking like this?" I cried. I knew that if I tried hard enough, I could have removed the tangles, but I wanted Daddy to think that I couldn't. Of course, Daddy knew at once what I was up to, but he agreed anyway that I should, indeed, have my hair cut.

Thelma and I made appointments at the hairdressers in the Broadway down past Lyon Road, and we both decided we would like the Italian cut that was very fashionable at this time. Thelma and I emerged from the hairdressers, both feeling like Elizabeth Taylor with a curl above each eye.

16

A DANISH TRIP

OUR TRIP TO DENMARK IN AUGUST 1956, MEANT A COACH RIDE from the club to Harwich, and a ferryboat from Harwich to Esbjerg in Denmark. The journey took nineteen hours. The strong winds across the water made it a very rough overnight trip.

Wendy, Sylvia and Evelyn on the ferryboat

Huddled in our bunks, we rocked back and forth while the pounding waves tossed the boat about like a cork. We could hear the cargo sliding around in the hold as we tried to sleep in tiny bunks in a cramped cabin. We were all very physically sick, so the smell of that, coupled with the smell of the diesel oil, didn't help either. I was feeling terrible as two of the girls, and Thelma, enabled me to get up to the deck of the ship, thinking that some fresh air might do the trick. As they struggled to get me up the stairs, against the rolling of the boat, we passed two of the sailors. They had 'seen it all before' and thought it was hilarious and laughed at us. But I had never felt so bad. I thought I was going to die. As I leaned over the deck rail, watching the grey waves rising and falling, I threw up, and that was where Miss Tee found me. She suggested that I came below and ate something, then I would feel better.

That was the last thing I wanted to do. I didn't think I could manage to eat anything EVER again, but I was willing to try something to get rid of this terrible feeling of nausea. Down below, we sat around a large table in the dining cabin.

Two boys from our group were already sitting there. They had stayed up all night, believing that if they continually ate, they wouldn't feel sick! So, armed with bags of crisps and biscuits, they had stayed up and played cards. It appeared to be working for them. As the dining room was in the centre of the boat, it made sense, as we wouldn't feel the rolling as much as we had in the cabin that was on one side of the ferry.

I was getting settled at the table when the chef arrived. He proudly placed a massive pot of soup in front of us. It was green with what looked like raw fish floating in it! I took one look at the soup and staggered out of the door. I am sure he must have realized how awful it looked, especially to someone who had been throwing up! The boys all jeered and laughed at me as I made my way back to our cabin to lie down.

Finally, we reached port, and I was never so thankful than to get off that boat! A coach that would take us to our final destination in Helsingor was waiting for us on the dockside. By this time, although very tired from lack of sleep, I was starting to feel much better. The excitement of being on holiday was beginning to take hold!

Vapnagoord *(pronounced Wapnagoor)* was a typical whitewashed, Danish farm hostel, with steps leading up to a wide arched entranceway, which in turn lead to a large bright hall. We alighted from the coach together.

The farmer and his wife came to welcome us and showed us to our rooms. The girls were in one wing, and the boys were in another. Thelma and I had a double bed that looked out onto a garden that sloped down to a duck pond.

A vast expanse of lawn dotted with shrubs made up the garden with fields and pasture beyond. We unpacked our clothes and put them away in the wardrobes and chest of drawers provided for us. Then we found our way to the dining room.

It was a very pretty pristine room decorated in blue and white – we all fell in love with the décor and the freshness of it all. The meals served at the farm were terrific. They were tasty and delicious in the Danish tradition, and we looked forward to each mealtime with relish. I loved the creamy milk from the dairy herd served for us for our breakfast cereal, and the smell of the freshly baked bread as it wafted up to the bedrooms each morning as we awoke.

After we had eaten, we decided to explore the grounds and the immediate area. We passed homes with huge windows and lots of houseplants on the windowsills, something we were not familiar with at this time. I thought it a lovely idea!

At the end of a short path leading beyond the duck pond, Thelma, Sylvia, Evelyn, Sybil, and I discovered a small, secluded beach. We called it our exclusive beach! Exclusive except for a boy named David Smith that had developed a crush on me, followed me everywhere, much to my embarrassment and annoyance. He would sunbathe there at any given opportunity.

On Monday, a coach arrived to take us on a trip to visit Copenhagen and Rosenborg Palace. We were allowed to see the Crown Jewels and Danish Regalia. The statue of Hans Christian Anderson, which stood in the King's garden, reminded me of the fairy tales I had read growing up.

On the first Saturday, all the girls had been invited to the local dance where, it seemed, a whole garrison of Danish soldiers had arrived. Apparently, word had got around that some girls from England had arrived. The English boys all stayed behind at the farm. We had a marvellous time and hardly sat out for a single dance. I made a new friend, his name was Dieter, he was tall and lean and blonde, and he made me promise to write to him. But I am afraid, fascinating as he was, that it was a promise I didn't keep. I suppose it was a case of 'out of sight, out of mind.'

Meanwhile, back at the farm, the boys decided to get even with us for deserting them. So they went around the farm grounds collecting baby frogs the Danish called them 'dacs.' These creatures were everywhere. While we were at the dance, the boys took these tiny, slimy creatures and filled the girls' beds, wardrobes and chests of drawers with them. Finally, in a final act of defiance, one of the boys had stolen a pair of knickers from a girl's chest of drawers. He climbed the flagpole and hung them as a trophy, right next to the Danish flag.

We came home from the dance laughing and chatting about the great time we had had. Upon entering our rooms, the laughs soon changed to screams as we were faced with baby frogs jumping about at every turn. They were everywhere. They jumped out of the drawers, the wardrobes and even from under the duvets. So now it was the boys' turn to laugh, and laugh they did at the ensuing screams!

In the morning, though, the tables turned again when the farmer remarked angrily at the audacity of the boys. It was an insult to hang a pair of girls knickers from his flagpole and next to the Danish flag! The boys were banned from ever entering the girls' dormitories again, and Miss Tee was not pleased either and told them they would all face punishment when we got home. Though she said it for the benefit of the farmer, I suspect that she secretly saw the funny side of the episode.

We went on lots of sightseeing trips. Thelma and I were fascinated at how many of the people we saw were blonde. I suppose with Thelma and I being dark-haired, their blonde hair seemed more noticeable to us. Their hair was a beautiful pale gold colour. They also all spoke perfect English, which was just as well as none of us knew Danish – apart from "Tak" (thank you) – or "Mange tak" (thank you very much.)

Wendy in Denmark

We visited Fredensborg Castle; it was a beautiful building and the summer residence of the Danish King and Queen. We marvelled at the boy soldiers dressed in their striking blue uniforms. The guide showed us where our Queen Elizabeth had scrawled Lilibet (her father's pet name for her) on one of the windows with a diamond ring when she came for a visit with her parents.

Then we toured the beautiful ornamental gardens. We also visited the Tivoli Gardens in Copenhagen, gazed at the Pagoda, and swooned over the lovely aromas coming from the coffee shops. We took pictures standing beside the Little Mermaid statue, we boarded a barge and were fascinated by the sights from the canals. We saw the Tuborg Breweries and were amazed to see the wagons drawn by horses wearing hats with holes cut for their ears!

Sixth row back on right. Denis, Brian, Wendy and Thelma. Evelyn, Sylvia and Sybil behind. 1958.

We also visited Fredericksborg Castle, erected in the 17th Century in the Renaissance style. After it burned down in 1878, it was rebuilt and made into a national historical Museum with money donated by the Danish Carlsberg Breweries. The rooms in this castle were lavishly decorated, with very ornate ceilings, and on the walls hung tapestries and paintings of Danish Royalty.

We stopped for lunch at a fantastic restaurant, where we discovered redcurrant jelly. The food in Denmark was delicious, and everything was so artistically displayed on the dish. The presentation was everything to the Danes. Here we were treated to a buffet of amazing Danish treats. We thought the redcurrant jelly was for dessert, so filled our plates with it, adding some cream, much to the amusement of the Danes. It turned out that the jelly should be eaten with the meat!

We returned to the hostel, and as it was late, we all went straight to bed. The next day Thelma and I went into town and discovered a small jewellers shop in one of the back streets. We gazed in the window, and I noticed a beautiful bracelet singled out on a stand. The bracelet was made with tiny silver and blue enamel butterflies. It seemed to beckon to me, and I fell in love with it and quickly purchased it. When I got back to the hostel, I proudly showed it off to the other girls, and they all fell in love with it also.

The owner of the jewellers was delighted when I returned with my friends, and the girls purchased his whole stock of enamelled bracelets!

One day we took a trip across the water to Helsingborg in Sweden. Then boarded a coach to Malmo. It was to be a quick trip if we were to catch the ferry back to Denmark. We couldn't be late for supper!

Thelma, Wendy, Sylvia and Sybil

Of course, we couldn't miss seeing Kronborg castle – of Hamlet, Prince of Denmark fame, in Ellsinore. Although we tired of the boy who kept reciting, "There is something rotten in the state of Denmark," and, "and on the right, we have a brick factory!"

We loved how clean everything was in Denmark – there was no litter anywhere. In all, we had a wonderful time, and for our first trip abroad, it was a definite hit! It was only to be expected that we would become friends with the boys with all the teenage hormones floating around. Most of the girls paired off with the boys. Thelma and I became attached to two boys, we had a lot of laughs with them.

It was during our second week at the farm that the shocking news came from Brian at home to say that Daddy had had a heart attack and was in the hospital!

Thelma and I were very shocked and thought that we should go home right then. But Brian told us that there was nothing we could do and that Daddy was well looked after, so we decided to stay until the end of the holiday.

The news did mar the rest of our holiday, and we couldn't wait to get home and see how Daddy was. Thankfully, he did recover and was allowed home a week later. As he wasn't allowed to climb the stairs now, we had to buy a single chair-bed for him. It was a dark green moquette, and we placed it in the living room. Soon began a more difficult job for Thelma, looking after four teens PLUS an ailing father.

After about six months of recuperating, Daddy was allowed back to work. He was so glad to get back to normal. This change released Thelma from staying at home, so she got herself a job with an Optician in town. Thelma had been going to evening classes at the Technical School for typing, so she was able to fall into office work. It was a bit more humdrum and a significant change from sewing for the 'high and mighty.' She also became interested in Amateur Dramatics held at the Congregational Church and was forever reciting her lines. "Oh Gregory, don't be such a grouch, what could be more entertaining!"

Thelma and I loved going to the cinema, and we went to see 'South Pacific' five times. It was in 'Todd A.O.,' an American post-production company founded in 1953, providing sound-related services to the motion picture and television industries. For more than 5 decades, it became the worldwide leader in theatre sound.

We couldn't get enough of both the film and the music, and especially Rossano Brazzi. We never failed to get the latest copy of the 'Film Review' from the attendant walking around the Cinema, who would cry, "Film Review, sixpence each."

17

JUDY'S STORY

One evening we were all sitting around in the living room. Thelma was busy crocheting table mats with pretty coloured pansies around the edge. I was knitting and David and Christopher were playing Monopoly. Brian was playing records on the record player, and Daddy was clearing out his desk drawers. "Ah, here it is, this is what I was looking for, this is for you." He handed me a typed letter it read:-

North Detroit Street,

Hollywood, California, U.S.A.

October 15, 1935

Dear Arthur,

Yes, it was Judy – and even yet after all these months, we can hardly make ourselves believe it is true; it seems that each time a car pulls up in front, she will come bursting in the front door with a cheerio and a kiss. Well, I must not get started talking about her – I don't need to tell either of you what her going means to Mummy, Doug, and me and to Billy. We do get a crumb of comfort from the fact that all her twenty-six years on earth were happy ones – she had never known any serious pain or sorrow – and the last six months were by far the happiest of all. I could tell you many things about her, for she had developed in the last four years wonderfully and few young women, I am sure, ever had more loving friends. They all were fond of her, high and low – she had the happy faculty of being at home with everybody. She had some splendid friends at Paramount and was invited to the homes of the really big folks in the studio – they liked her; it didn't matter that she was not one of them in position. Stars, directors, and executives – they came to pay their last respects and sent her lovely flowers. I suppose I am bragging, and it's not very decent of me – but we were so proud of her. Well, I won't say any more.

I think, on the whole, we all are standing it very well indeed; we don't allow ourselves to mope, nor does Billy; each tries to keep cheerful for the others, and that helps us all.

About a month after her death, we had so many enquiries that it was literally impossible to write details to everyone, so I made one account and typed a lot of copies, one of which I am enclosing. It pretty well tells the whole story, and there isn't a lot I can add except to say that Billy has been back at work for several weeks, gets about nicely with some limping and a cane. The knee and ankle will be entirely all right eventually; it developed from the X-rays that the side of his skull was fractured and he still has some trouble with that, and also his eyes bother him, but the specialists assure him that that is all the result of the severe blow and nervous shock and that he will be perfectly all right in time.

He has been working frightfully hard, sort of drives himself, I guess, to help forget and to tire himself out so he can sleep. His Chief, Louis D. Lighton, has made a very fine contract with M.G.M and went over there a few weeks ago, leaving Billy to finish their last two pictures, "Peter Ibbetson," and "Collegiate," after which Billy will also go to M.G.M. He hates to leave Paramount after so many years there, but he and Mr. Lighton work so well together and have such a high regard for each other that he thinks it wise. And we think that he rather wants to get away from Paramount where everything reminds him of Judy.

Mr. Lighton and Billy have turned out some very fine pictures for Paramount, the last of which, "Lives of a Bengal Lancer," was rather exceptionally good, and if you saw it, I think you will agree. Billy had almost entire charge of it, and I saw a lot of it being made as, on several occasions, I went with Billy and spent some days on the various locations in the mountains. It would all interest you perhaps but would make a pretty long story. At M.G.M., they expect their first productions will be Kipling's "Kim" and "Captains Courageous."

It might interest you to know that the Government investigation of the crash resulted in the carrying company being heavily blamed on several counts and accused of taking unnecessary chances in several ways. Nothing went wrong with the plane itself – a big cabined, double-engined cruiser. A U.S. Senator, a young girl, and the two pilots were killed practically immediately; Judy died some hours later; and the Paramount electrician, Mr. Drew, eventually had to have his leg amputated; the other Paramount men are now all up and about but still not entirely recovered from their injuries. The young girl, by the way, was a sister to the ground man at Kansas City who ordered the plane on, and the mother and other relatives were waiting with him at the airport for the plane. There would unquestionably have been more deaths had Billy not been able to get help; Drew, Wallace and Wing couldn't have lasted out any more hours as they were in an isolated section and might not have been found for a long time.

There's no news of ourselves except that we are all well in health. I can't begin to tell you how grateful we are for your letter; I didn't try to notify individuals, and the folks in England all seemed to have got it from the papers or somehow, yet even over here some of our friends didn't know about it at first, so you mustn't consider it strange you were in ignorance. We realize how you feel for we know how genuinely fond you were of Judy – and she of you.

Your change of address means I do hope that you have got something to do that is worthwhile; anyway, when you can drop us a line and tell us the news of yourselves – and I hope it is good.

Mr. and Mrs. Bryce are about the same in every way and would send their best wishes if they knew I was writing.

We all join in regards and good wishes to your wife, you and the girls.

I turned the page and read on:-

As there are many details connected with this tragic experience of Judy and Billy, which we feel our relatives and friends would like to know about, I shall try to set them down as briefly as I can and, at the same time, not allow my feelings to get the better of me. It would be too much of a task to write long letters to each one.

On Sunday afternoon, May 5th., Helen, Douglas and I drove out to their home in Westwood Village. We picked them up and took them *over to the airport at Glendale – and saw them off happy and smiling at four o'clock. They were due in Washington, D.C. the next afternoon. Billy's work - he was a producer in charge of a group that were to do about four weeks' work on a picture at the Naval Academy in Annapolis, Md. – would probably keep him extremely busy there and in Baltimore and Washington, so depending somewhat on what developed after arrival, Judy planned to spend some time in New York, having obtained four weeks' leave of absence from the Studio. She was not, therefore, being sent out officially by Paramount, as were the other five men - Billy, Mr. Wallace, the director, Mr. Wing the business manager, Mr. Drew head electrician, and Mr. Sharp cameraman. Other members of the unit, stars and others, were to leave a few days later.*

The first word we received of trouble was at eight o'clock the next morning – Monday- when the Studio telephoned that the plane had crashed in Missouri, some 1600 air miles distant – 2000 by rail – but that no definite news had yet come through. The word was that Billy was slightly hurt, and Judy uninjured. All reports confirmed this up to about noon when suddenly the story changed, and the news was that Judy's back was broken and that she was paralyzed from the waist down – and that she was in a very serious condition. This turned out to be the truth.

Paramount immediately set their large organization in motion and had specialists and nurses, equipment, etc., sent out to the little country hospital from Kansas City, 160 miles away, and did wonders in caring for their people. Plans were at once on foot to get relatives out there, and seven of us left from the same airport only twenty-four hours after Judy and Billy. We had good flying weather, and the trip was uneventful; we arrived at Kansas City, Mo. at 2-30 a.m. (Central Time), doing the 1500 miles in just eight hours. From Kansas City, we had to motor 160 miles to

Macon – heavy fog all the way – and reached there at 7:00 a.m. And there I learned that Judy had died at two o'clock that morning – May 7th.

The story of their terrible experience is that they got into the fog some 150 miles before reaching Kansas City; could not land at the airport there and were ordered by the K. C. ground man to proceed and try to make a small emergency field 135 miles farther on – which the pilot failed to locate. Presumably, he was completely lost; there is a Federal investigation going on, but nothing of consequence has been made public yet.

Most of the passengers were dosing apparently, not knowing the real situation. Bill's first intimation of trouble was the sight of a small white schoolhouse, which the plane just missed – he still sees it flashing past his right eye. Immediately the warning light to fasten set belts was put on, and he got Judy's fastened, put his arms around her in an attempt to hold her – then the crash and he remembers nothing for a few minutes. His left ankle was broken, the right knee injured so that it buckled under him, and the right side of his head badly smashed and bleeding profusely; many other minor cuts and bruises. He evidently landed on the side of his head in the mud – it was a farm field – and undoubtedly that saved him a broken neck or crushed skull. It was, of course, pitch dark- about 3:30 a.m. – but he called and stumbled about until he located Judy.

Nearly everyone was thrown from the plane – a large all-metal cruiser but smashed to bits – some as far as fifty or sixty feet. Judy was conscious but could not move – a man lay across her, but Billy managed to get him off. He realized from the fact that her legs were helpless and without feeling, and a pain in her back, that she was severely hurt. Then he heard the baby crying – a child of sixteen months – and eventually found her under a pile of debris; got her clear and put her with her mother, who was very badly hurt and is still I understand in a serious condition.

Meantime one woman, the only passenger unhurt, was wandering about in a somewhat dazed condition; Billy saw a light rather hazily, one eye being blinded and the other covered with blood, which he hoped was a house, but the woman insisted it was a beacon light miles away; so he finally turned in the opposite direction. He crawled and stumbled across fields and ditches, eventually finding a house, which proved to be vacant; then he heard a dog barking in the distance, and by calling in order to keep him barking and following the sound eventually came to another house. He then discovered that the woman had been following him – and she remained at the house so far as he knows.

The farmer there had a broken arm, but he started back to the house near the wreck where Billy had seen the light – the only one within miles with a telephone. But he sent his two little boys in the other directions for help, and his wife and Billy took a lantern and blankets and went back to the plane. The farmer's wife took the baby, and the lantern back to one of the houses, and Billy was alone again, trying to make the others as comfortable as he could with blankets. Everything was very wet, but he found bits of dry wood from the plane, matches from one of the dead pilot's pockets, and started a small fire. By that time, farmers began to arrive, and all were carried to the nearby house, and a little later, first aid came from a village five or six miles away. It was about eight o'clock when the first ambulances arrived, and gradually the injured were got to the little hospital in Macon, a small town; but they had to drive eight miles over a muddy, rutty road, and then ten miles on a paved road.

Three of the Paramount men were in grave danger for several days; one almost died, but they are all out of danger now, and all are back in Los Angeles except one, Mr. Drew, who is still in Macon. At first, Billy was of course given slight attention as he was not in a serious condition; in fact, his ankle and knee were not fixed, except for temporary bandages, until after I got there; but they were anxious about his face and eye and had given them proper attention. He has been back three weeks, in Cedars of Lebanon hospital, and is recovering splendidly and apparently completely; the ankle and knee are all that keep him in bed, and he will soon be out. He is coming to live with us, and while he has been laid up, we have broken up their lovely home, putting everything in storage except what was needed for his use here with us, until he can bring himself to decide what he wants to do with his and Judy's things.

But as for Judy, X-rays showed a badly crushed vertebra, which looked hopeless, and by the evening of Monday, it was decided to operate as a forlorn hope – on the bare chance that the spinal cord was not injured. They telephoned here to Helen and Douglas, and she talked with Billy, who was satisfied for them to go ahead but wanted our consent also; and the doctors said they dared not await my arrival. They operated at once but found that the cord was completely severed – and that was the end; they could do nothing. Late in the afternoon preceding the operation, they put Billy and Judy in her room, and they had their last hours together – she was kept fairly free from pain. Judy dictated, to one of the paramount men there from Kansas City, a cheerful and hopeful message to us. He showed me the scribbled copy he took down and said he intended to keep it as long as he lived – that to him it was the greatest badge of courage he had ever known, as she knew she had almost no chance; but she told the doctors and Billy that she preferred death to a few months of life as a helpless and suffering cripple.

Her bravery, cheeriness and fortitude through it all – the only serious crisis she had ever been called upon to face – make us almost ashamed of our own grief. The specialist told me that in all his experience, he had never seen a woman show so much spirit and courage. When she left Billy to go to the operating table, of course, he broke down badly, but she only smiled and even whistled at him to cheer him up. The head doctor of the hospital told me with tears in his eyes that when she died, everybody, doctors, nurses and all, broke down – a thing he had never before seen in a hospital – she had so endeared herself to them in the eighteen hours she lay there. Nurses cried when they talked to me, even the farm boys who carried her to their home cried in telling me about her, and the ambulance driver who brought her to Macon. Perhaps I am saying things I should not – but we may be forgiven, I think, for feeling proud of her. Billy did not want me to bring her back until he could come; but although he was not fit to stand the journey of 2000 miles by train, the doctors consented that he leave on Thursday the 9th, and we all left then - Billy, his sister who had gone out there with me. Judy and I – and Billy made the two-day trip comfortably. The head of the Studio and two of his associates, with Douglas and Billy's brother Irving, met the train about sixty miles out and rode in with him; and they arranged to get him off at Pasadena, to avoid reporters at Los Angeles; and he was driven direct from there to the hospital here.

Judy's funeral was impressive, and all Paramount nearly was there, from the top down to gatemen; the chapel where the services were conducted could not hold all who came, nor could they get all the flowers inside – they tell us there were ninety-six floral pieces. Part of it was due to respect for Billy of course, but we had not realized before how much real affection there was for Judy herself – When one of the most outstanding men in the industry shows marked emotion at the funeral and tells a friend of ours that he looks upon her passing as a great personal loss, it is an indication of how genuinely fond they all were of her.

Following the public services, there was a private commitment service at Forest Lawn Memorial Park, Glendale, where Judy's body was cremated. I cannot finish without a word of appreciation and admiration for the way the Paramount officials spared neither pains, expense, nor effort to do everything in their power for their injured. On our trip home they had doctors board the train at five cities en route to check up on Billy's condition; they even had this through transcontinental train stopped at a little way station twenty miles north of Macon, to save him the long drive to Kansas City; they have sent Mr. Drew's children out there to be with him and his wife – they have thought of everything and stopped at nothing. And they paid all expenses of every kind – even all personal telephone messages to Los Angeles. And though Judy was not sent east by the Company, but was accompanying her husband, the heads of the Company, both from New York and here, telephoned that they would consider it a personal favour if Billy would permit the Company to pay all Judy's funeral expenses – that's the kind of folks there are in the picture business.

I have tried to write with but one thought in mind – to let those who loved Judy know all the details that would be of real interest to them. If it reads sort of cold-blooded, I am sorry, but I dare not write about it in any other way - the whole thing is too fresh in my mind, and too much of a nightmare for any other way of telling the story.

I looked up with tears in my eyes.

“Judy was a very special person,” my father began, “so we thought we would name our next girl after her, and so that is why we named you Wendy Judith, it sounded better than Wendy Judy, but we just wanted to honour her memory.” He said, hugging me and brushing away my tears. “Keep the letter and remember her,” he concluded, closing the desk drawer.

How lovely to have been given the name of such a courageous woman, I hoped that I could live up to such an honour.

18

TWO NEW JOBS

AS TIME WENT ON, I DECIDED THAT I DIDN'T WANT TO WORK AT Hides any more, I had had enough of buttons, and so I applied for work at a small shop about four doors down from Hides. It was called 'Wheeler's Library' and was a small lending library at the back of the shop. On the right-hand counter, they sold newspapers and magazines, and on the left-hand side, they sold embroidery fabrics, silks and wools.

Two elderly sisters and a middle-aged woman ran the shop. The oldest woman was very tiny and wore long black skirts, black Victorian boots, a pair of pince-nez, and with her hair in a bun. Pince-nez is a style of glasses, popular in the late 19th and early 20th centuries, that are supported without earpieces, by pinching the bridge of the nose. The name comes from French *pincer*, "to pinch," and *nez*, for "nose." She reminded me of Queen Victoria, She had a lovely smile, and she used to eat jars of calves' foot jelly for lunch 'for her health.'

The old fashioned phone intrigued me. It had a piece you held to your ear, and the part you spoke into which was on a long stem, I thought, looked like a daffodil. I didn't stay long, however, although the ladies I worked with were all very kind to me, in the end, I missed having the young company of my friends at Hides. So I decided I would find a job in London.

Daddy wasn't keen on me working in London. He didn't think it was safe and had tried to dissuade me from doing so. But by this time, both Sylvia and Anne had each found themselves good jobs in London. Sylvia was working for Penguin Books near St. Paul's Cathedral, and Anne was working with a diamond company in Holborn. I wanted to join them, as the pay was so much better and offered more excitement than merely being a shop-girl in Bexleyheath. So Daddy relented as there was a job advertised in the Evening News for a coupon clerk at the Anglo American Corporation of South Africa, situated at Holborn Viaduct. So, Thelma decided to take me there for my interview.

On the day of the interview, I dressed very smartly. I felt very confident in my beautiful turquoise wool coat that Thelma made for me, and I felt very confident with my hair, that had grown long again, tied back in a ponytail.

Unfortunately, on the journey between the Station and the office, it poured with rain, and so we both arrived soaked to the skin and looking like two drowned rats. Luckily, the two men giving the interview had looked past my appearance, for they gave me the job.

I was to be working in the coupon department on the second floor, dealing with the shares coupons.

Now, working at this job, I could meet up with Sylvia and Anne, and we could travel on the train to and from Bexleyheath Station together. It made Daddy happy that I would be going each day with my friends.

I enjoyed the walk of a mile or so to the station every morning, passing my old schools, to meet up with my friends, and board the crowded train to take us to Cannon Street Station. From there, I would walk past the impressive building of St. Paul's Cathedral until I reached my office in Holborn. I loved the architecture of the beautiful Cathedral with it's imposing dome and impressive entrance designed by Sir Christopher Wren.

After work, we made that journey in reverse. I walked past the bombsites still yet unbuilt, along by St. Paul's. Sometimes they were practising bell ringing. The great bells rang out, and the sound travelled a long way. How I loved listening to them. One moment I would be walking along the road with the noise of the traffic in my ears, and then I would turn the corner and hear nothing but the bells. It was so uplifting.

I enjoyed my job even though, after a while, it was boring. I liked the men and women I worked with, and we all got on quite well. Working in the coupon department proved to be a monotonous job - entering the numbers from the shares coupons by hand into huge ledgers. Gladly, I found that I could enter the figures and daydream at the same time! I was well paid, receiving ten pounds a week, which was an enormous raise after the two pounds seventeen shillings a week I had earned at Wheeler's Library. It was just as well, as now I had my train fare to afford.

There were two girls about my age, three older women and three men in my office. We had a tea lady who came round at the same time, morning and afternoon, with the tea trolley so that we could drink it while we carried on working. She would give us all a cup of tea with four wrapped lumps of sugar in the saucer. I only used two pieces in my tea and would save the rest in my desk drawer. Then, when I was feeling hungry, I would eat them. In the time I was there, I collected a full drawer of sugar lumps.

All employees were treated to a delicious free three-course lunch in the canteen each day. There were always three choices of starter, entrée, and dessert on the menu, which also included a salad. There were cheese and biscuits to follow the dessert with tea or coffee. It was an excellent meal.

We always sat at the same table seating four people in the canteen. One day, as there was only one empty seat when I arrived, I found myself sitting at a table with three elderly men, at least they seemed old to me. At first, I felt shy sitting with them and couldn't think of anything to say, but they were very friendly and treated me like their daughter. Some of the other girls thought I must be a bit odd to sit with three older men, but I didn't care; I thought they were charming!

I had discovered a very nice hairdresser shop close to the office. I decided to go for an 'oil treatment' that left my hair looking wonderfully shiny. One of my co-workers was a photographer on the side. He offered to take my photo. I was pleased with the result.

My coworker's photography

At Christmas, we were given 10% of our year's salary as a bonus. One Christmas we were treated to a dinner dance at the Savoy Hotel in the Strand. The following year we went to the Dorchester Hotel in Park Lane – the expensive part of London. We were allowed to get ready in the ladies' washrooms at work. We rode in a limousine to the Hotel. I had gone shopping for a new dress for the occasion. It had short sleeves, a sweetheart neckline, and the fabric was multi-coloured flowered taffeta on a black background. It had a tiny waist and a full skirt. So I was able, again, to wear my full blue petticoat underneath. I wasn't quite sure whether the dress was quite "me" when I purchased it, but the sales lady assured me it was "just you." So, assuming she knew what she was talking about, I bought it.

19

TRAIN CRASH

ON DECEMBER 4TH, 1957, I WAS AT WORK AS USUAL. I HAD BEEN working for the Anglo American Corporation for three years now. I had become accustomed to meeting up with my friends Sylvia and Anne, at Cannon Street Station each day on the way home to Bexleyheath.

On this particular day, the fog, which had hung around most of the day, was going to get thicker. My boss had received word from the Managing Director that we could leave earlier if we wished. So I put on my coat, grabbed my bag, and went on my way.

Every day for three years, I would walk with my coworker, John, a short walk along the road from the office to Holborn Viaduct Station, where he would get on the train, and I would continue walking the long walk to Cannon Street Station to meet up with my friends. On this day, with the fog so thick, I took a wrong turn and found myself climbing the stairs at Blackfriars Station instead! To this day, I cannot recal the journey between leaving John at Holborn Viaduct Station and arriving at Blackfriars Station. Very weird!

I could have caught a train at Holborn Viaduct Station as the next station from there was Blackfriars, so it made no sense to walk to Blackfriars Station. So, now I would need to take a different train to Bexleyheath. I decided to stay as it was beginning to get dark. I didn't feel comfortable walking in the fog and the mist made everything damp and forbidding.

There were only a few people in the station. I sauntered along the platform staring at the ground to guide me, still trying to make sense of why and how I had got here, when I literally bumped into a girl. She seemed familiar. She turned out to be Phillipa Noel, an old school friend from Bexley Technical School!

After leaving school, Phillipa Noel had emigrated with her family to Australia. Now she was in England visiting other members of her family for a while. What are the odds that I should bump into her at a Station in London, especially as I wasn't meant to be at this Station? I never did find out what she was doing in the city. The area was predominately offices at this time, and it would have been more likely that she would have gone to the West End if she were shopping. It was all rather extraordinary.

Our train pulled slowly into the Station, and as Phillipa and I got on together, chattering away, a young man also got into our carriage and sat opposite us. He was the typical City Gent with a dark suit and rolled-up umbrella, which he placed in the overhead luggage rack. We were the only people in this carriage. Chatting happily about our school days and the girls and teachers we remembered, we paid him little attention. I got out my knitting. I was making a sweater. Knitting was my favourite pastime while travelling on the train, to while away the long journey.

It was still very foggy and now completely dark outside. I remember that we had to go through Nunhead and several tunnels before we would reach Lewisham. We would have to cross over the Viaduct and join the Dartford line, to finally get to my stop at Bexleyheath. There was a lot of stopping and starting on the journey as we moved slowly through Nunhead.

After yet another long stop, we were moving along slowly again. Suddenly with squealing brakes, the train pulled up quite sharply, throwing us all forward. All the lights went out.

There appeared to be a commotion further down the train, and I said, "I thought I heard someone say we have to get out." "Well, I'm not getting out," said Phillipa, "we aren't even in the Station."

Out of the gloom, a pale face wearing a peaked cap appeared at our window.

"I am your driver," the man said. "We have a bit of bother up ahead, and the train can't go any further. You will have to get out and walk back to Nunhead Station. You will be all right." He continued, "the electricity has cut out." And with that, he moved on to the next carriage to inform another set of travellers.

We assumed that something must have fallen onto the track blocking our way. "Well, I don't fancy walking through the tunnels," I said, turning to Phillipa.

The young man sitting opposite said, "let us get out, I will help you," and he took my arm.

So, together with the other passengers, we jumped down onto the track in the pitch darkness. It seemed strangely quiet as we began to shuffle along in a single file, back along the line the way we had come. It all seemed surreal, with the fog muffling our voices.

I was feeling somewhat scared, and by this time, there was a long procession of people walking along the side of the track beside the train. A voice from somewhere behind us called, “Has anyone lost a ball of wool?”

I realized it was mine, and I sheepishly retrieved it and stuffed it into my bag. We all laughed, which broke the tension a bit. The young man who had introduced himself as David said,

“If you don’t want to go through the tunnels, we can climb up the bank here.”

We were not sure if the electricity might come on again at any moment, so David bravely said jovially

“I will put my umbrella on the pipes, and if I fizzle out, you carry on along the line to Nunhead.”

So, David gingerly placed his rolled umbrella on the pipes and wires running along the side of the rail track while Phillipa and I stood back. Nothing happened, so, taking my hand, David helped me up the bank. He then took hold of Phillipa’s hand, assisting her over the pipes at the side of the track. Then with David bringing up the rear, we all made our way through the long wet grass to the top of the bank, leading to someone’s back garden.

All the while, there was silence, apart from the passenger’s hushed talking as they helped and encouraged each other up the steep damp grassy bank in the darkness. All the time, the fog was swirling eerily around us.

As we drew near to the house, we discovered a hole in the fence and climbed through. A dog began to bark and hearing the noise; a man came out from a side door. When we explained what we were all doing traipsing through his back garden, he showed us the way to go and then stayed and directed the other passengers out to the road.

By this time, we could hear many ambulances with their bells ringing frantically. The fog was so thick that you literally couldn't see your hand in front of your face, and we concluded that there must have been an accident due to the fog; somehow, I didn't connect it with 'our' train.

We approached a stationary bus, "Come on," David said, "let's get on this bus."

"We're not going anywhere," said the driver standing by the bus with his arms folded. "It is too foggy to travel."

"Well, we will just have to walk," announced Phillipa resignedly.

So we started to walk. I was glad to have my companions with me. David seemed to know the area well, so he was able to guide us through the maze of streets. I hadn't a clue where we were, and I noticed the strange eerie silence as there was now no traffic noise. Indeed, there was nothing on the roads at all, and all the while, the fog swirled around us. Phillipa and I chatted about school and the friends we used to have.

"This is my road," David suddenly announced, "Keep following this road, and you will eventually reach Welling." Then, disappearing into the fog, he was gone. I was sorry to see David go. Somehow, his presence had made me feel safe.

We were now walking towards Shooters Hill. I jumped as a car came at me out of the fog and mounted the pavement about six inches from me. Luckily, it was travelling slowly. The driver stuck his head out of the window. "Sorry ducks, I thought this was my turning." He said, cheerfully.

"Well, you should look where you are going," I snapped unreasonably, my heart thumping.

What a strange journey this was turning out to be, I thought, and thank goodness my Guardian Angel was watching over me. Little did I know just how well I was being guided.

Phillipa and I continued, now in silence. Would this journey ever end? I wondered. We trekked first up and then down Shooters Hill and eventually reached Welling. The fog had somewhat lifted by this time, and we noticed that the buses were running here. We must have walked about eight or ten miles.

Phillipa was staying with her family in Welling, so we said our goodbyes and I hopped on the 696, just as it was leaving the bus stop. I never saw or heard from Phillipa again.

I arrived home to a worried Thelma. "Where have you been? I have had dinner ready for hours," she exclaimed.

"Our train broke down in the fog," I replied, "and we had to get out and walk. Where's Daddy?"

"He's not home yet either, so perhaps he is walking too. Are you all right?" Thelma asked, concerned.

I was hungry and tired, and as I devoured the food she put in front of me, I told her what had happened.

Daddy usually caught a later train than me, and as he worked in Leicester Square, he came via CharingCross Station. We turned on the radio to listen to the news, "News is coming in of a train crash in Lewisham," the announcer reported. Thelma and I looked at each other with our mouths open. So THAT'S what had happened!

Still unaware of how close I had been to dying that night, I voiced both our thoughts when I said,

"I hope Daddy is alright."

Just then, in answer to my unspoken prayer, we heard the familiar sound of Daddy's key in the lock. There he was, tired like me, but unharmed. We hugged him tightly.

The Lewisham train crash turned out to be one of the most significant disasters in rail history. It transpired that a Charing Cross to Hayes train had stopped on a red light near Lewisham Station just beyond the viaduct, which carried the Holborn Viaduct train to Lewisham. Unfortunately, the following Cannon Street to Ramsgate Express train, because of the fog, collided with the back of it, pushing it into the bridge support of the Viaduct, which then collapsed on top of the train. The Driver had missed two preceding signals in the fog and so was unable to stop.

The driver of our train was fortunate that he was going slow enough to see the twisted metal girder from the damaged viaduct bending upwards towards the carriage. So, he was able to stop the train before going on to the bridge; otherwise, our train would have landed on top of the other two, turning it into a triple train crash.

There were 90 people killed and 173 injured that night. The bodies of the dead were laid out in rows on the Lewisham Station platform.

I took the following day off from work to get over the shock, and because I couldn't face getting on a train again. When we met up the next day, Sylvia told me that her train had stopped right opposite the crash site, as the power had automatically turned off when the crash happened. She told me that the train was so crowded that she had to stand, squashed against the window, unable to move, while watching and listening to the cries for help from the injured passengers. Some of whom were hanging from the rafters of the bridge to where the impact had projected them. It was a sight and sound that she would never, ever forget.

How was it that I was spared all of this? For Phillipa, David and I, the fog had absorbed the sound of the passengers' cries, and so we saw and heard nothing. I thanked God that I was spared from witnessing the horror. But what about David and Phillipa? Were they the angels sent to guide me home, I wonder? I believe that they were.

20

BOYFRIENDS AND HOLIDAYS

As I went to the youth club several times a week, and now that I was twenty, it was inevitable that I should eventually find myself a boyfriend. I took a shine to Ted. He reminded me of James Dean with his blonde hair and similar ways. One evening after club, he offered to walk me home. So we caught the bus from Shenstone Park to the Clock Tower. We held hands and chatted all the way, Unaware of the time, we dawdled along. Upon turning the corner of Pelham Road, I looked up to see my father standing at the gate waiting for me. Imagine my horror. Ted took one look at Daddy's face, turned, and left me.

Upon reaching our gate, I saw Daddy's grim look as he said, "Where have you been?" Without giving me a chance to answer his question he said, "Get inside."

Once we were inside the house, he turned to me, "You are supposed to be home by 10 o'clock! Now you will stay in for the next two weeks."

Although it must have been hard for him, being both mother and father to me, he had worried when I didn't return home at the prearranged time, and then to see me with a boy was simply too much for him to tolerate. Poor Daddy.

I didn't understand his severe reaction and I angrily stomped upstairs.

"I hate you!" I shouted at him, "and I hate you!" he shouted back.

But I remember that I felt secretly pleased that he cared so much. I did not hate him, I was just mad.

Eventually, when I was allowed to go back to the club, I met up with Ted again. He had bought himself a motorcycle, and it was wonderful to sit behind him. Neither of us wearing a helmet, we raced along the Rochester Way. We had lots of fun, but I soon tired of him once he became keen on me and decided to kiss me. I did not like being kissed.

It was about this time that a new flower shop opened up by the clock tower. It was called Wendy's, which seemed to me like an omen. I would press my face to the shop window, trying to pluck up the courage to go and ask for a job. It reminded me of my cousins' flower shop in Peckham, where I stayed after Mummy died. However, when I told Daddy about it, he said to me that working in a damp atmosphere would make my asthma worse, so, reluctantly, I gave up the idea. All the same, I really would have loved to have worked there. I loved flowers and plants. Working in the garden was my idea of heaven. But I accepted that Daddy must know best.

One day a new girl came to work at our office at Anglo American. Her name was Betty, she was very pretty with short, blonde, wavy hair. She was always smiling. I took an instant liking to her, and we became good friends.

That year, 1959, the youth club was going to visit Germany for the summer holidays. We were to be staying in a Youth Hostel in Westphalia, which was near the Hertz Mountains. Thelma wanted to remain at home to look after Daddy. She took her job so seriously. So, I persuaded my friend Betty to come with us. Betty's mother was not too happy about her daughter going to Germany, and made me promise to look after her. I said that I would.

The German youth hostel in the town of Herford was run by an ex-German soldier with only one hand. Apparently, his right hand had been severed by Russian soldiers when the Germans invaded Russia during the war. (Would we ever be able to forget the war?) I wondered why he ran the youth hostel, he was a large bald man who didn't seem to be overly fond of British teenagers, and he never seemed to smile.

All the girls slept in one dormitory in bunk beds, and all the boys in another. Before we left England, we had been told to take breakfast cereal with us, and also tea, as it would not be provided. The first morning we had our Weetabix for breakfast, and there were rolls with jam. The tea was made in the pot together with the milk already added. It was cold, and it tasted awful. Dinner consisted of cabbage water soup and German sausage. Both were horrible.

We went on many trips. One such trip was to the Hertz Mountains, where we had our photo taken with a man dressed as a bear.

Sybil, Betty and Wendy with the bear

We visited the restored Mohner dam that was once destroyed by the bouncing bomb dropped by the dam busters during the Second World War. As we were having our photos taken sitting on the top of the dam, I was wearing a lilac gingham full-skirted dress with, my puffy blue waist slip to make the skirt stand out. The boys had all purchased Robin Hood type hats with feathers in them. My group met up with some British soldiers stationed nearby. They took photos of us together.

On the Mohner Dam

Wendy and friend Betty on the Mohner Dam

We also went to Teutoburgerwald and gazed at the enormous statue of 'Herman the Great,' pock-marked from British aircraft fire, again from the war; it was so difficult to forget about the war.

We visited the border between East and West Germany and went up to the fence that separated the East from the West. Armed guards stood in their towers on the other side of the barbed wire fence, and the considerable width of bare earth was regularly raked and inspected for footprints. People were shot if they were caught trying to escape to the other side. The people in the village on our side of the border were upset that some of our boys reached through the wire to touch the earth. Understandably, they were afraid of repercussions from the border guards.

On Thursday, we visited the Bundersgartenshau in Dortmund with its vast gardens with chairlifts and futuristic railcars to ferry us to other parts of the gardens. Betty and I took a walk along a path. We were busy chatting together when we heard some classical music. We hurried along to see where it was coming from and came upon a clearing by a lake. There were rows of seats facing a theatre, but what caught our eyes were the huge dancing fountains that rose from the lake, in time to the music. It was quite spellbinding. We sat for a while to listen and the seats filled up around us with more spectators.

Then we got chatting to three German girls who spoke excellent English. Two were named Doris and the third, Brigitte. They were the first Germans I had struck up a conversation with since the two little German Jewish girls came to our school after the war. I remember that it felt odd to realize that German girls were just like us and not at all the monsters we had been led to believe. It was quite a memorable day.

German Girls Doris, Brigitte, with Wendy and Doris

Near to the town of Herford was a British garrison. It didn't take the soldiers long before they discovered that there were some English girls in town! Eve, Sybil, Betty and I made friends with three soldiers, and they took us to see many more of the sights.

John from the club and three British Soldiers

We thoroughly enjoyed ourselves, and on the day we were due to leave, we were sitting in the back garden of the hostel chatting. I didn't notice that the other girls had gone to get ready to catch the coach, leaving me talking to the boys. Somehow the girls didn't see that I was not with them until the coach reached the airport, and they realized that I was not there.

Shortly after the coach had left, I discovered that I had been abandoned. I was annoyed and worried until one of the soldiers offered to take me to the airport on the back of his motorbike. Luckily for me, our luggage had been stacked in the hall, so my case had gone with all the others in the coach. I don't know how I could have balanced it on the back of a motorbike! I was thrilled that I got to ride on the back of the bike. You should have seen the girls' faces as I roared up on the motorcycle clinging to the back of a handsome soldier. The looks on their faces made it worth being left behind! The rest of the club members ribbed me for flirting and Miss Tee told me off, in no uncertain terms, but I think she was feeling guilty for not noticing she was one passenger short!

I was not sorry to be going home as I thought the food was awful, and I was famished after two weeks of inadequate food, as were we all. I had sent Thelma a postcard saying,

Dear Thelma,

So glad to receive your letter. It didn't matter about the tea and coffee (I had forgotten to pack mine) as Betty gave me her extra tin.

I'm so sorry the boys forgot your Birthday, but I hope my present will make up for it.

We arrive at Victoria on Sunday at 7 a.m. and before I forget, could I have a nice square breakfast? The food here is terrible. Today I have eaten three rolls, butter and jam and lukewarm coffee for breakfast, potato soup and cold tea for dinner, and custard for tea and those are the best meals so far.

Anyway, I'll see you Sunday.

Love Wendy.

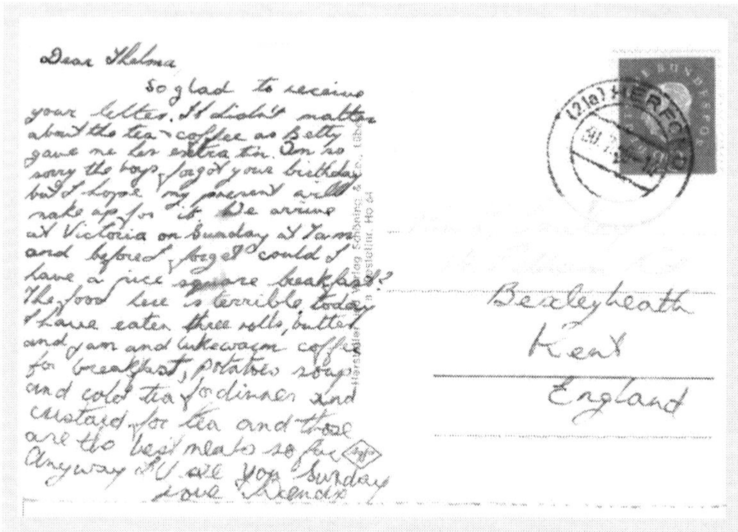
Dear Thelma
So glad to receive your letter. It didn't matter about the tea & coffee as Betty gave me her extra tin. Am so sorry the boys forgot your birthday but I hope my present will make up for it. We arrive at Victoria on Sunday at 7a.m. and before I forget could I have a nice square breakfast? The food here is terrible, today I have eaten three rolls, butter and jam and lukewarm coffee for breakfast, potatoes soup and cold tea for dinner and custard for tea and those are the best meals so far. Anyway I'll see you Sunday
love Wendy

Bexleyheath
Kent
England

Postcard to Thelma from Wendy

It had been quite an experience and, in many ways, lots of fun, but I was happy to get home again.

Upon my return I learned that Daddy had had another heart attack while I was away. Thelma hadn't let me know, as she didn't want to spoil my holiday. He seemed okay to me when I hugged him, though his lovely dark hair had turned white overnight!

In September, it was my twenty-first birthday. Daddy gave me a box of Pond's make-up. In the box were pots of vanishing cream and cleansing cream, a lipstick, eye shadow and some mascara. So, I supposed that now he wouldn't mind me wearing make-up. He also gave me a brown leather purse.

I was allowed to have a few friends for tea, so I invited Sylvia and Miss Tee from the youth club. I liked Miss Tee, and secretly I hoped she and Daddy might hit it off, but it wasn't to be.

Thelma gave me a beautiful crystal necklace, and she also had a cake made for me in the shape of a basket of roses. It was beautiful and a shame to cut it. Brian gave me a pretty blue manicure case, and his two friends, Donald and Keith, made me a metal key in their workshop and gave me an unusual vase, it was black, with a picture of Pegasus, the flying horse.

The people at work were very kind, and I received lots of cards and a beautiful Marcasite brooch and earrings, and a gorgeous pottery table lamp, from the gentlemen whom I sat with at lunch.

Wendy's twenty-first birthday

In October, I was busy working in the coupon department at Anglo American with my two lady bosses Miss Copper and Miss

Star. We were amused when Miss Copper announced that she was getting married and that her fiancé was Mr. Steel!

Miss Star sang in her local church choir and had a thing about Tommy Steel, the rock and roll singer. She was always singing his latest hits.

> *"Oh I never felt more like singing the blues*
> *I never thought that I'd ever lose*
> *Your love dear, why d'you do me this way?"*

Betty and I remained friends even when she was transferred to the third-floor typing pool. As I was on the second floor, I didn't see her much, especially as we took our lunch at different times.

21

GOODBYE DADDY

One October evening I arrived home from work to find Daddy peeling the potatoes for dinner. He seemed tired and kept sighing as he did them. Selfishly I didn't offer to help him and went to watch the television. That night Daddy was suffering from chest pains, but he kept it to himself, as he didn't want to disturb us. By morning he asked me to phone the doctor as he was concerned about his heart. I went next door but one to Mrs. Clayton's and asked her if I might use her phone. She wasn't too pleased, but she allowed me to use it. However, her attitude softened as she heard me calling the doctor, who said he would send an ambulance straight away.

In a daze, as the seriousness of the occasion slowly filtered through to my still sleepy brain, I returned and told Daddy they were sending an ambulance for him. I can see him now, still pulling faces to try and make us smile as they loaded him into the ambulance in a sitting chair. I can remember thinking foolishly that we were all standing in order of age as Thelma, Brian, myself, David and Christopher stood by the side of the road to wave goodbye to him. We were all upset to see Daddy go, still, I got myself ready for work and went to meet Sylvia and her friend Marie with whom she worked. We met up as usual, together with Anne, on the platform of Bexleyheath Station. On telling them what had happened about Daddy going into hospital, I burst into tears.

At the office, I went through the motions of working, and I am sure many of the coupon numbers got entered in the wrong places yet again.

That evening after work, Thelma and I went to visit Daddy in the hospital. Echoing our mood, the rain was coming down in buckets, as it had been all day, as we caught the bus to the hospital. He was in Joyce Green Hospital just outside Dartford. We found Daddy, looking very pale and propped up on pillows, fast asleep. He had wires attached to his chest and arms. Thelma and I sat either side of the bed, chatting and watching him, but he didn't open his eyes. I am not sure he even knew we were there, and eventually we left after kissing him goodbye.

The journey home was a bit of a nightmare; the constant rain had caused flooding, and although I was wearing high heels, the water was above my ankles. By the time the bus arrived, the water was lapping over the running board as the driver skilfully maneuvered through the flooded streets. Thelma and I were two very wet and depressed looking individuals when we finally arrived home that evening.

The following days we took it in turns to visit Daddy. On the last visit I made on October 21st, he was awake but didn't say much, as he lay with his eyes closed. A male nurse came to remove his wires and ripped the sticking plaster from his arm. Daddy yelled as the plaster tore at the long hairs on his arm. I glared at the nurse.

"Sorry," he said apologetically, "It's the only way to do it. It would be more painful for him if I were to do it more slowly."

All too soon, the nurse rang the bell for the end of visiting hours. It was time for me to leave and as I kissed Daddy goodbye and hugged him, he opened his eyes. Still thinking he was at home, and that I was going out, he said to me, "Don't be late back."

The following morning 22nd October, Brian woke Thelma and I who were sleeping together in the double bed in the back bedroom. "Mrs. Clayton just knocked," he began and then without a pause, "she said Daddy died in the night."

It was a shock to be awakened like this and I started to laugh hysterically, then the laugh turned into weeping. Thelma was numb, and looking at me she said, "I can't cry."

I don't remember much about the next few days. I know that I went to work that morning, and again I burst into tears as I met Sylvia and Anne at the station when they asked me how Daddy was. A woman standing next to us remarked to her friend, "That girl is always crying." She must have overheard me after Daddy had first gone into hospital.

I can't imagine how Thelma arranged the funeral, but I suppose she must have had help from Sheila and Betty. Everyone at work was very kind, and I was allowed the day off to go to my father's funeral. It was the first funeral to which I had ever been. We had the funeral flowers stacked up in the hall as they were delivered, and I can remember the smell of the Chrysanthemums. To this day, I don't like that smell because of the memories it invokes.

At the Congregational Church, I can remember sitting in the front row with Daddy's coffin an arm's length away. It seemed like a nightmare that my Daddy should be inside this box. How I wanted him to cuddle me and tell me everything was all right, but I knew it could never be. We all sadly followed the coffin from the church, as if in a dream.

"Oh, Daddy, why did you leave us?" I loved him so much, and now he was gone. He would have been 65 years old that December.

Daddy was place into the funeral car and the procession of cars made their way to the cemetery behind Christ Church in the Broadway. We all alighted from the vehicles and followed behind the coffin to my mother's graveside. Daddy had told us that he wanted to be buried with Mummy even though she was in the unconsecrated part of the cemetery, saved for those who were unbaptized. It didn't matter to him; he wanted to be with his only love.

As we stood around the gaping hole, the vicar began his prayer. I started to sway. I wanted to jump in to be with my parents.

Betty standing opposite saw me and said, "Grab her."

Thelma grabbed hold of my arm and steadied me. She stood with her arms around me as the Vicar came to the end of his prayers.

After the service, the cars drove us home, and I don't remember what happened after that, except that one of Daddy's workmates came and said how sorry he was and how Daddy would be "sadly missed at the office."

I thought to myself. "He is already sadly missed here."

No one could have had a kinder, more loving and caring father than mine.

"Dear Daddy, I will always love you."

22

TRUE ROMANCE

Now, there was only the five of us — twenty-six-year-old Thelma, Brian twenty-three, me aged twenty-one, David eighteen and Christopher at fifteen. I began to help Thelma more with the ironing, though it wasn't much fun ironing three lots of shirts and darning three lots of socks. Before I had decided to help, it must have been tough on Thelma, how selfish I was, not to notice how hard she worked to look after us.

Daddy hadn't made a will, as he didn't have anything to leave, except the house and the furniture. There now began a dispute between Sheila and Brian as to who should inherit the house. Brian thought that being the eldest boy, it should go to him, whereas Sheila being the eldest child, thought she should have it. If the house were to belong to either of them, Thelma and I wondered where WE would live. Worrying about this, I found it hard to concentrate at work. I was continuously admonished for putting the numbers in the wrong place in the ledgers. The now, Mrs. Steel and Miss Star had the job of checking everything we entered in the enormous ledgers, they found it simple to find my mistakes.

One day I went into the office, and Mrs. Steel beckoned me over. "I have a nephew in Canada," she began, "he has written to me asking if I could find him a pen friend, would you be interested in writing to him? "Yes," I answered, "I would like that." I loved to write. So she gave me his address, and I started writing to Sam Chevers from Niagara, Ontario.

The first letter he sent me was all about his home. Then he told me that he had joined the army and was going to be stationed in Germany, and that maybe we could meet up if he could get the time off.

I was very excited at the notion of meeting a Canadian, and so I wrote back and told him I would love to meet him one day. We wrote to each other for some time. At Christmas, I received a parcel, which contained a lovely white angora scarf and mittens together with a golden necklace and bracelet.

Finally, he managed to get some leave. Sam had sent me a head and shoulders photo of him so that I would recognize him. So I invited him home to meet the family. He was intrigued at our houses with their boundary fences and hedges. "In Canada, our homes don't have fences, they are all open, why do you have so many fences?" I was sure I didn't know.

I took Sam for a walk-in Martens Grove, and as we climbed the steps by the tennis courts, he turned to me and landed a smacking wet kiss on my mouth.

"Will you marry me?" he asked.

It took me by surprise. I didn't like the kiss, and I certainly didn't want to marry this boy.

"Oh," I said airily, "I am not ever getting married."

We didn't seem to have much to say to each other after that, and so he left, and I suppose eventually went back to Canada, for I never heard from him again.

Working day after day at Anglo American became boring to me, having to enter numbers in a ledger was not my idea of fun anymore, and so I decided to learn shorthand and typing. My bosses were keen for me to take this step and paid for me to attend Pitman's College in Southampton Row. I got on well with the typing but found the shorthand daunting and couldn't see the point of learning the dots and dashes, to begin with, only to unlearn them as I progressed. So I dropped out of the shorthand class.

No doubt, my employers wanted to take advantage of what I had learned, for I was transferred to the ground floor of the building, to the computer room. The I.B.M. computers were huge noisy machines, and my job now was to be a punch card operator, putting cards through the machine and typing holes in them, representing the information each card was to convey. Each batch of punch cards went through a sorting machine. Then from there, into huge printing machines that churned out yards and yards of paper and shares certificates. Some were to be mailed, and the rest were put in boxes and sent to the archives in the basement.

I was working in an office with twenty-six other girls, whose foul language I had never heard before, and to which I didn't enjoy listening. I didn't fit in with them, and after five years of working for Anglo American, I decided to leave. As a leaving present, they presented me with a lovely cream coloured suitcase.

For my next adventure, I decided that I would like to try and get a job as a clerk/typist and so I went for an interview at a solicitor's office. After being interviewed, the Solicitor and I both decided that it wasn't for me, so I signed on at an agency to do some temping work instead.

Thelma and I decided we would go dancing every Friday night, so we began to attend dances at the Embassy Ballroom in Welling. I enjoyed these outings and sometimes we met up with Sylvia and Anne. We would dance together when we couldn't find a male partner, and we had great fun jiving together. We would put our bags on the floor and dance around them.

Shortly after that, Thelma and I joined the Sunday dance club at the Yorkshire Grey in Eltham.

On Sunday, March 26th, 1961, I had been off work with the flu all week. I was feeling fed up with being stuck indoors. I wanted to go dancing, but Thelma didn't feel like it, so I decided I would go on my own. I dressed in my favourite dress of the moment, as I thought that it showed off my curves. It was a pink Courtelle, slim-fitting shirt waister with a tie belt. I fixed a pink porcelain rose clasp at the neck and put on matching pink rose earrings. Splashing 'In Love' perfume behind my ears, I said goodbye to Thelma and the boys and caught the bus to Eltham. I didn't feel guilty about going dancing. I was feeling much better, and I thought that when I went to the doctors the following day, he would be sure to sign me off.

It was unusual for me to go anywhere on my own as I always felt too shy, but this evening I felt different. I stood in the ballroom as the music played, and looked around the room. After several dances with various young men, I noticed the young man standing in front of me. As I gazed at the back of his neck, I liked what I saw, the short hair and smart dark suit. For some reason, I said to myself, "I am going to make you fall in love with me."

Suddenly, as if my magic spell had worked, he turned and asked me to dance. Earlier, (I found out later,) he had noticed me dancing and had positioned himself in front of me so that he could be the first to ask me to dance as soon as the music began. The dance was a quickstep, the dance that I had practiced many times at school. He was whirling me around the floor in the most professional way, until the music stopped. Brian introduced himself and asked me if I would like a drink. I decided on a Babycham, so with our glasses in hand, we made our way to the chairs and tables at the edge of the ballroom.

"Where did you learn to dance like that?" I asked him as we sat down. It was quite a change to have a partner who could dance. "My parents teach ballroom dancing," he replied. "Where did you learn?"

"At school." I smiled at the recollection of dancing with another girl in the hall at the Technical school. But I was happy that the experience taught me how to ballroom dance properly.

Brian seemed nice, quite a gentleman, which made a nice change from some of the boys I had met. He told me he was "on leave from his job in the Merchant Navy, as the Second Electrician on the Gothic, one of the Shaw Saville passenger ships."

Having always had a thing about sailors, I was pleased that I had met this one, who seemed to enjoy chatting to me. We talked and danced some more, and at the end of the evening, as we danced the last waltz and he held me in his arms, he asked me if he could give me a lift home. Somehow I felt safe with him, so I agreed, as I was not too keen at the thought of catching the bus alone at eleven o'clock at night (something I had not considered when starting out on my trip.)

We went out to the car park. Brian had hired a car for his leave and had another week left before he had to get back to his ship. Like a perfect gentleman, he held the door open for me before getting into the driving seat. As he drove me home, I took a sly sideways look at him, and I liked what I saw. The way he had his hair combed and his handsome profile in the streetlights. Not to mention the gorgeous back of his neck that I had noticed when he stood in front of me in the dance hall. I told him that I had been off work with the flu, and that I had to go back to the doctors tomorrow to be signed off so that I could return to my work with the Agency.

"Well, that means you have tomorrow off work. How would you like to come out for a drive with me afterwards? I could come over and pick you up after you have seen the doctor." He said with a smile.

I liked that idea, so we agreed he would come over.

When we reached my home, and he parked the car, I asked him if he would like to come in for a cup of tea. He agreed and we went into the house.

We walked into the front room, where Thelma, who had just washed her hair, sat in front of the fire in curlers. As we entered, she looked up and, seeing Brian, she turned red. "Oh, Wendy, how could you?"

Brian grinned, and I laughed as I introduced him. He thought Thelma was my mother (but apologized to her when he realized his mistake.) David and Christopher looked at each other, and David whispered, "I suppose we will have to cut yet another notch in the doorpost," referring to the fact that I had bought 'yet another' boy home. I frowned at him, but the remark went over Brian's head, either that or he chose not to hear it.

Despite him seeing her in her curlers, Thelma decided that she liked Brian. He stayed a while, and when we said goodbye at the front door, he kissed me on the cheek.

The next day I went to see the doctor who, to my amazement and joy, decided that it would be a good idea if I had another week off work. Brian was very pleased about that when I told him though I felt a tad guilty knowing that I had gone dancing when I was not considered fit enough to work. However, the guilt gradually disappeared as each day that week Brian would drive up in his hired car and whirl me off to yet another new place. I had a great time going to the seaside and all manner of other exciting places.

I was enjoying his company and being taken out for meals. We seemed to think alike. I remember asking him to identify something and he called it "a wimwom to wind the sun up with." That was a saying Daddy used to have, and I had never heard anyone else say it. How strange was that?

On Saturday, Brian and I decided to go and visit Kew Gardens. When I mentioned it to Thelma, she invited herself and David and Christopher came along too. (I think she wanted to keep an eye on me.)

Brian was happy to drive us all there, and when he came to call for us, he handed me a box of Dairy Box chocolates. How nice was that? However, once we got to the park, David and Christopher proceeded to eat them all between them! Brian and I didn't mind, we were too wrapped up in each other to care.

David and Christopher eating Dairy Box chocolates

Brian and Wendy with Christopher

Brian and Wendy at Kew Gardens

Wendy and Brain 1961

Later, Brian took me to his home in Eastview Avenue, Plumstead to introduce me to his parents. His home was similar to mine but was a semi-detached house on a hill. He had a stepmother he called Nell and she lived there with Brian's father, Jack.

Jack and Nell welcomed me warmly and seemed very nice. To be helpful, I offered to put the kettle on to make us all a cup of tea. I filled the kettle, put it on the electric cooker, turned on the hotplate, and returned to the backroom to join the others. Shortly afterwards, there was a smell of burning and I rushed into the kitchen with Nell close behind me; we discovered flames licking around the feet of the electric kettle. I was used to using our gas cooker at home. I felt so stupid that I had ruined their kettle, although they made a joke of it. All the same, I could imagine what was going through their heads at my stupidity. It certainly didn't do much for a first impression!

By the end of the week, Brian and I had become firm friends. Brian was due back to his ship on Saturday and would be sailing to New Zealand, a trip that would take him about three months.

"So, will you write to me?" he asked after kissing me with feeling, on the lips this time.

I told him I would, though I had no deep feelings for him. On our first trip to the seaside, I had bought him a plastic blowup kind of monkey creature, called a Cuddleybug, which we christened Godfrey for some reason. Brian told me he would keep it with him in his cabin to remind him of me while he was away, and off he went.

So my new friend was gone, though I wrote to him, I wasn't missing him too much. Thelma and I continued to visit our Sunday dance club in Eltham and sometimes on a Friday night we went dancing at the Embassy Ballroom in Welling, again meeting up with Sylvia, Sybil and Anne.

23

JOURNEY TO SCOTLAND

I SUCCEEDED IN LANDING A JOB IN AN OFFICE IN THE CITY OF London for a company called 'The Chair Selection Centre.' It meant that now I would be getting off the train at London Bridge and catching the tube into the City. I was working in an office all by myself, answering the telephone and typing correspondence. This time I felt lonely, as it seemed I was their only employee. Two partners owned the company. They advertised their garden chairs for sale in the Sunday papers.

My office was really only an address for the mail and cheques. Sometimes the janitor of the building would come and spend the time of day with me. He would reminisce about the war. He told me, "During the Blitz, an incendiary bomb dropped on the building just opposite, and it burned to the ground. Many people lost their lives, there was nothing we could do to help them." The people of London suffered so much during this time.

When answering the telephone, I started getting angry phone calls from the people who hadn't received their chairs, demanding their money back. One of my bosses would turn up each day to collect all the cheques. I told him about the phone calls and how I was concerned that these people had not received their chairs. He told me not to worry about it. Shortly afterwards, he and his partner gave up their office in the city, favouring the building next to the chair factory. They thought it would be a good idea if I moved there too, thereby saving them the rent they paid for their city office.

My new office, now situated in Highgate in North London. Being at the end of the tube line, meant an even further journey for me. It also would mean an increase in fares.

On my first visit to Highgate, I caught the train to London Bridge, where I was to change and get on the underground to Highgate. Once the the train stopped, I climbed down onto the platform. “Hm,” I thought, “that platform is a long way down.”

I seemed to be the only passenger that had alighted there, and while I proceeded to walk to the Exit, I heard a wolf whistle, “Well,” I thought again, indignantly, “I’m not taking any notice of you!”

When I reached the end of the platform there was no exit. I realized that this was the platform used only for the mail. I turned to see the porter, the one who had whistled at me, standing holding the carriage door open with his hand on his hip. Feeling very stupid, I quickly ran towards him and, with his help, climbed back up into the carriage, through it, and alighted on the other side of the train.

I walked along the platform with a red face, giggling as I pictured the looks on the passenger’s faces as I came in one side of the carriage and out of the other. I felt like the comedian Tony Hancock.

The factory and office building of 'The Chair Selection Centre' was right beside the viaduct, where occasionally, people had the urge to jump off the bridge to the road below.

Fortunately, the Whittington Hospital was only just along the road. Also along the street from my new office was Highgate Park, where I would go and take my sandwiches at lunchtime. After I was full, I would feed the birds and squirrels there. The gardens were lovely, so it made a nice break.

One day, as I wandered along the paths, I came across the Aviary, where they kept a talking toucan named George. George would amuse the passers-by with his shrill wolf whistle, and then he would say, "Allo! Ows yer Farver?" in a strong cockney accent.

I shared my small office with another girl, Mandy. She wore false eyelashes and would mutter "I love men," in a husky voice. She kept me in stitches. She also worked on the switchboard in this tiny office. One day I was asked to operate the switchboard while Mandy went to lunch. That day I had a sore throat and a touch of laryngitis, so I was also speaking with a husky voice. This bug was going around the office.The Managing director also had it.

I was very unfamiliar with the workings of the switchboard. However, I managed to put two customers through to each other and felt a sense of accomplishment. Then, I cut the Managing Director off in mid-sentence. He came out and ranted and raved at me, displeased. With his sore throat, he rasped that I had cost him an important call. In my own raspy voice, I tried shouting back at him, trying to explain that another call had come through, but he wouldn't listen. It must have sounded quite funny for an outsider to hear us croaking at each other.

'The Chair Selection Centre' had a showroom in Oxford Street in the West End of London, and I found myself transferred there. Thanksfully, it made my journey much more manageable, and it was lovely to go shopping in Oxford Street in the lunch hour.

An elderly couple, Mr. and Mrs. Denham, ran the showroom, and I got on with them quite well. The only problem was, there wasn't much office work to do. So, I ended up selling chairs, which wasn't my idea of fun. I soon realized that they couldn't afford to pay me and, as I hadn't been paid any wages for two weeks, I was getting fed up and frustrated with the situation. So I decided to cut my losses and leave. So I went back to the agency again.

The agency didn't have any suitable work for me at this time, so I decided instead, to go and stay with my eldest sister Sheila at her home in East Kilbride in Lanarkshire, Scotland.

I embarked the coach and travelled by myself on the overnight trip. I slept a little, but not enough. We stopped at about three a.m. to 'stretch our legs,' and then continued to Glasgow. Sheila met me at the coach station. I was feeling somewhat washed out, though I had enjoyed the journey, especially seeing the sheep with their lambs, and the rising sun coming up over the Scottish hills.

Sheila now had three children, Janet aged six, who had an imaginary friend, Stephen aged four who had a teddy bear he called Mr. Edward Bear, and Adrian 3 months old. According to Janet, her imaginary friend kept tying himself to the banisters and Sheila had to pretend to untie him.

On one particular day, Sheila had gone to the hairdressers, leaving me to babysit. I put Adrian down for a nap, then I went to make a cup of tea. Stephen was playing in the garden with his friend Craig. However, Stephen got annoyed when he couldn't understand Craig's broad Scottish accent, so they began to fight. Stephen called Craig a 'sissy' because he was wearing a kilt, and as they began to punch one another. I had to separate them, and sent Craig home in a huff. Stephen came indoors, wiping his eyes and feeling cross. So, I picked him up, sat him on my lap and hugged him.

"Why don't you tell me a story?" I said, to take his mind off Craig.

He began, "One day Mr. Edward Bear built a great big airplane, and he took lots of people for a ride in it. But the people pushed him out."

"Poor Mr. Edward Bear," I said. "Still he had a parachute, didn't he?"

"Yes," replied Stephen, "but it didn't work, and when he landed on the ground, another airplane ran over his shoes."

I said, hiding a smile, "Oh dear, so he had flat shoes, then what did he do?"

"He went and bought some high heels!" said Stephen.

We both laughed. After I had finished laughing, he told me with a serious face, "I am not going to marry Fiona 'cos she wants a maid to do her work, and maids are expensive. I am going to marry Rosemary instead 'cos she doesn't want anything." What an imagination this small boy had.

I had begun taking more of an interest in gardening. Daddy had planted a Laburnum tree by the side of the corrugated iron

Anderson shelter, now out of the ground. He also planted a pink flowering currant shrub. He had built a wooden bird feeder, so we planted some daffodils and small plants underneath, making a small flowerbed. I extended the flower bed from there, along Mr. Mepham's fence, using his beautiful climbing roses as a backdrop. In the flowerbed on the other side of the square lawn, I planted some Lupin seeds. We had kept the chickens on this piece of ground, and although the chickens were long gone, they had left us excellent fertile soil. I was amazed at the many coloured, giant Lupins that emerged in that space. Each day I would go and water the seedlings and couldn't believe how tall they were growing. I would gaze at them, completely enthralled. So, it seemed that gardening was my all-prevailing interest at this time. I also loved to pick the flowers and arrange them – sometimes arranging four or five vases and placing them around the living room.

My brother Brian, on the other hand, was into radios, and it was about this time that he decided to concentrate on all things electrical. He built himself a radio with a 'cat's whisker' so that he could listen to Radio Luxembourg. He also got himself a job in the local radio store in the Broadway. Somehow, without us noticing, he had become very talented. Like me, he missed a lot of schooling because of his asthma, and because he used to skive off on occasion. He finally came to his senses when he left school and started to pay attention to his education by attending evening classes at Woolwich Polytechnic.

He had been keen on a girl named Kathleen, a Roman Catholic, and he decided to join her church so that he could see more of her. Brian brought Kathleen home to meet us, and I became friends with her. We would go to the Yorkshire Grey dances together, and we got on well. So much so, that we planned to take a skiing trip to Austria together.

They used to hold dances at the Woolwich Polytechnic at weekends, and it was at one of these that my brother Brian met a nurse called Val. He fell hook line and sinker for her. It wasn't long before they were going steady, and we were not surprised when Brian announced that they were to be married.

24

A BRIDE FOR BRIAN AND A BOYFRIEND FOR THELMA

CHRISTOPHER HAD BEEN WORKING AS AN APPRENTICED PLUMBER to Howard Hitchcock's father, who lived around the corner in Woolwich Road. Thelma had a bit of a crush on Howard Hitchcock, who was tall and handsome, but too old for me.

Howard was working on his car one morning as I went to work. He had parked it right where I crossed the road to go to the station, so I think he must have somehow seen me go that way and positioned himself to bump into me. As I went to pass him, he stopped me, and we started chatting. I told him about the youth club and how we sometimes went ice-skating. We talked for a bit, and then I went on my way to work. A couple of days later, there he was again. This time he asked me if I would like to go ice-skating with him. Now I thought, "Thelma has such a crush on him and would kill me if I went out with him," so I said, "I will go with you on one condition." "Oh, what's that?" he asked with a big smile. "That my sister Thelma comes too." He looked serious for a moment, but he agreed. So that was settled. I was very proud of the way I had engineered a meeting for

Thelma. When I got home and told her, she said,"Oh, you are joking." Then, "Did he say he would take us both?"

"Well, I don't want to go with him on my own," I replied, "He is not my type," I added, smiling to myself. She was over the moon.

So, Howard drove us to Streatham ice rink. I sat in the back so that Thelma could sit next to Howard. We went skating and hiking together several times, and Howard even agreed to drive us to Hastings when Thelma and I went on Holiday there.

Thelma and I had a lovely time in Hastings. When we arrived, we found a charming Bed and Breakfast place, dumped our bags and went out to see some of the sights. We visited the ruined castle that dated back to 1066. In the dungeons we noticed hollows in the walls and were told that they were made by prisoners as they were being tortured. Eeuw!

We visited the fishing boats and sampled freshly caught fish. One time we walked along the cliff path in the middle of a thunderstorm – probably not a good idea, but it was awe-inspiring. We sunbathed on the stony beach, and went to the cinema. It was a great holiday and did us both good to be away from the boys for a while. Although I think Thelma was missing Howard.

With brother Brian and Val's wedding fast approaching, I was thrilled when Val asked me to be a bridesmaid, together with Val's sister. She chose a beautiful sky blue brocade for our dresses, and of course, Thelma was going to make them. It was the first time I had been a 'proper' bridesmaid – being a bridesmaid at Sheila's Wedding didn't count.

Thelma took great pains to make our dresses a perfect fit. I looked stunning in this beautiful dress with its short sleeves, fitted bodice and three quarter length skirt. After the ceremony, when we came out of the Church, the photographer lined us all up for a Wedding picture. Unfortunately, he had been drinking and, as he backed away to get us all in the frame, he fell over backwards into a water fountain, ruining his camera at the same time. Sadly, we never got any pictures of Brian's wedding. What a pity nobody else thought to bring a camera.

At the reception, David's friend was sweet on me, "You look like a little blue Angel," he told me. I was not impressed, and spent a lot of time trying to avoid him. Besides, I was writing regularly to boyfriend Brian now and receiving many letters back. My feelings for Brian were growing stronger as time went on.

At the end of the evening, brother Brian and Val left for their honeymoon. And so now there were four of us.

25

BRIAN RETURNS

It seemed that now David, Christopher and I could no longer live peaceably together. We were forever arguing and fighting. Poor Thelma was in the middle of it all. Finally, Ron, Sheila's husband, decided to take charge and told us it was time we all moved out, as Sheila was going to sell the house. (Sheila had finally won the argument)

"It's time you all moved on," said Ron, "my mother made us all move out when we were sixteen." He was referring to he and his brother and sister. He then disappeared, leaving us to think about what he had said.

Scared now, and missing our father, who had always been there for us after Mummy died, we began to argue yet again. One day things came to a head, so much so, that Thelma and I decided to move out and leave David and Christopher to argue without us. Our intention was to go for a couple of weeks just to give the boys a scare, so that it would make them think that they had best behave better towards us.

So, Thelma and I went to the council offices and got the names and addresses of the places that had rooms to rent.

We liked the two rooms that were in a bungalow in Horsham Road in Bexley. It seemed strange as we walked down Townley Road, as the last time I had done this was when I went to the Technical School. Thelma and I turned the corner into Horsham Road and reached the charming bungalow. It's garden backed onto the fields of the Technical School that we had both attended. Mrs. Batey, an elderly widow, owned the bungalow. She seemed very pleasant as she asked us questions about ourselves and our circumstances. After showing us around, Thelma and I agreed it was suitable. This was lucky for us as it was the first place we had viewed. We felt it must be right because it was number 14 – the same as our house in Pelham Road.

The old lady rented us her two front rooms – a sitting room and a bedroom. We shared the kitchen and bathroom with her, although she didn't like us using her kitchen. She told us that the rent would be four guineas a week and she would clean our rooms for us while we were at work. A Guinea was the equivalent of 21 shillings, so that worked out at 4 pounds 4 shillings a month. We moved in on September 30th, my 22nd Birthday.

After about a week, I went back to Pelham Road to see how David was getting on, only to discover that he was living on a diet of mashed potatoes because it was the only food he had in the house. He also told me that he had found some digs where he would be fed, and so would be moving out soon to enable Sheila to sell the house. I felt sorry for David, but I knew this would be a good thing for him, as he was getting so thin from not eating correctly. Meanwhile, Christopher had got a job training as a mental nurse at Dartford Hospital, and so he was being fed there.

So, Thelma and I settled into living with Mrs. Batey in her bungalow. It was certainly nice to have someone to clean up after us, though it meant that we didn't have much privacy. All the same, she was a sweet old lady.

As Mrs. Batey wasn't too keen for us to use her cooker, we tended not to cook very much. Every weekend Thelma and I lugged our laundry to the Laundromat up by the Police Station in the Broadway. Then, in the evenings, we would go dancing. Sometimes to the Yorkshire Grey or the Embassy Welling, and occasionally we tried the dance hall in Lewisham over Burtons.

At last, Thelma could enjoy a normal life without being tied to the boys and me. We both met several young men, though I wasn't keen on any of them. I was still writing to Brian, and we were becoming closer through our letters. I didn't want to hurt him in any way.

After three months away at sea, and during an unusually hot summer, Brian arrived home on leave. I was so excited at the thought of seeing him again. I wanted to look my best, so I dressed in a green floral silk pleated skirt and matching short-sleeved top, that came barely to the waist, and buttoned down the back. My white gloves, clutch handbag and high heels completed the outfit. I set out to walk up Townley Road to Bexleyheath Broadway. After catching the 696 trolley bus to Woolwich, I arrived at Welling Corner, where I got off and waited for another bus to take me to Plumstead, where Brian lived.

The second bus ride through Welling took me past box-like, prefabricated houses with 'pocket-handkerchief' gardens. They were built to be temporary homes for people bombed out of their homes during the war. But as time wore on, they became permanent homes and were still there twenty years later.

The final part of the journey after getting off that bus was a long walk up two very steep hills. Almost out of breath, yet filled with anticipation, I reached number 24 Eastview Avenue. I knocked on the door of Brian's home, stepped inside, and with his parents, eagerly awaited his return.

Sitting and waiting with Brian's stepmother, Nell, and her husband, Jack, I suddenly became apprehensive. "What if Brian had gone off me?" I thought. "Worse still, what if I didn't like him anymore?" My past experience in the romantic department was one of losing interest in a boy after just one week. I didn't like being kissed. "Would this turn out the same way?" I wondered. But then I remembered the beautiful letters he had sent to me while he was away. Every day, as I walked home from the station after work, there would be a letter waiting for me. "No," I thought, "I know that he is still interested in me."

The doorbell rang, and I rushed to open it. Brian stood there in his smart Naval uniform, looking more dashing than I had remembered. He came in, closed the door, dumped his bag on the floor, and we flung our arms around each other. I felt my temperature rising as he kissed me hard, on the mouth. Then, grabbing his hand, I pulled him into the dining room where his father and Nell were waiting to see him.

Nell smiled at my blushing face but didn't comment on it. "Put the kettle on." Brian said to me wickedly, with a twinkle in his eye. I blushed again, remembering the last episode with the kettle.

Nell had prepared a tea of tinned salmon and salad, with one of her incredible, homemade Victoria sponge cakes to follow. We sat around the tea table looking out of the window onto the flower garden. As we ate together, we were mesmerized by Brian's depiction of his travels to New Zealand and all the 'ports of call' on the way. As he spoke, I couldn't take my eyes off him, and I noticed that he had acquired a handsome tan from his trip at sea.

While we ate, Brian's father, Jack, interjected with some of his own amusing stories. Jack worked at Woolwich power station, and Nell would make his lunch for him to take to work. On one particular day he reached into the hall cupboard to get a carrier bag for his lunch, he slipped his lunch inside and set off for work. On arriving at work, Jack realized that there was a hand brush hanging from the handle of the bag and that he had walked there with this brush attached!

Another time, as a keen fisherman, Jack had boarded a bus, carrying his fishing rod, a tin of bait in his jacket pocket. He sat down and unbeknown to him, the lid of the tin came off. He looked down to see an army of maggots crawling out of his jacket pocket and walking across the seat!

Jack was barely five feet tall with a slim stature, and we laughed when he told us that his workmates called him Hercules, pronouncing it "Hercools".

After tea, Brian asked if I'd like to listen to his new L.P. I very much did! He took me into the front room, so that we could be alone, put the record on the Radiogramme, and sat beside me on the sofa.

The album was entitled "More. Johnny's Greatest Hits" and featured Johnny Mathis singing some of my favourite songs. It sounded beautiful and so romantic to me. I think my favourite was "Small World" because of the way Brian looked at me as we listened.

"Funny, you're a stranger who's come here, come
from another town.
Funny, I'm a stranger myself here, small
world, isn't it?
Funny you're a girl who likes children, that's an
important sign.
Funny, but I'd love to have children, small
world, isn't it?
We have so much in common.
It's a phenomenon..."

The words echoed our thoughts, and as Brian played a few more records, he stole a few kisses at the same time. We were getting quite comfortable, quietly listening to the music when he suddenly got up and threw a cushion at me. That did it; I knew now that I was utterly smitten with him.

While were were courting, Brian had asked me if I would marry him. My answer was "No!" I had made up my mind that I would not ever get married. I couldn't imagine living like my parents had, arguing all the time. I didn't know that marriage didn't have to be like that. Besides, now I had decided that I wanted to emigrate to Canada!

While Brian was away at sea, I had attended a meeting in London where they were trying to recruit new immigrants. I took all the information home to read. The idea intrigued me. I couldn't seem to settle into a job and thought it might be better to move away altogether, I reasoned. It would be nice to meet my Uncles, my mother's brothers whom she spoke of but I had never seen. For some reason, Canada seemed to beckon to me.

So the second time that Brian asked me to marry him, I said, “No, I have decided to go to Canada.” Though, after saying that aloud, I had a little doubt at the back of my mind.

While he was home, Brian introduced me to his friends Gary and Marion, who had married about five years previously. Gary also lived in Eastview Avenue, just across the road from him and Brian had, more or less, grown up with him. The two friends had also been in the Sea Cadets together and shared a love of the sea. One Saturday, with Gary and Marion, and some more of his friends, we all drove out into the country to a dance.

Brian told them that I was going to Canada, and they spent most of the evening trying to persuade me to change my mind. I think Brian had asked them to try to convince me to stay, but although I was very fond of Brian, I wasn’t going to let them change my mind. The thought of starting a new life was exciting and Canada was beckoning me.

After the dance. we were all driving in convoy down a hill. Gary and Marion drove in front, with Brian and I coming next, and the others bringing up the rear behind us. As we watched, Gary decided to start driving his sports car recklessly, Zig Zagging from left to right down the hill in time to the music playing on his radio. Fortunately for him, it was late, and there was no traffic around.

However, when he reached the bottom of the hill, there stood a burly motorcycle traffic policeman with his arms folded. Gary pulled over and was treated to a lecture on driving safely. Luckily the policeman forgave the behaviour and let him go with only a caution.

I had enjoyed meeting Brian’s friends, and some of their arguments against my emigrating had me questioning my stance.

On the next date with Brian, he drove me home, pulled up outside my front door and turned off the engine. He turned to me and said, "Well, are you going to marry me then?"

This was the third time of asking, and he was expecting the same answer as the last time he asked.

"Yes, I will marry you," I replied, smiling. My answer took him by surprise and then as he folded his arms around me, it was as though fireworks were going off. It was the strangest thing, but I am quite sure that I saw stars.

Secretly, I had previously decided that if Brian had asked me again, I would say "Yes!" It was an easy decision to make, as I now knew that I loved him hook, line, and sinker. We had met at the end of March, officially engaged by December of that same year. Even though he had been away at sea for three months at a time, and I hadn't seen too much of him, it felt right to be with him forever. Our many letters had helped us to get to know each other, and I knew in my heart that he was the man with whom I wanted to spend the rest of my life.

The next Saturday, Brian took me shopping for an engagement ring. As I gazed at the rings in Samuels Jewelers in Woolwich, my gaze fell on one beautiful ring. It cost forty pounds and was gold with a single diamond in a platinum setting. The design on both sides of the diamond looked like leaves, making the diamond look like a flower; it was perfect for me. We left the store and went back to the car. Brian placed the ring on my finger, and as we kissed, I felt so happy.

> *"Chances are, though I wear a silly grin, the*
> *moment you come into view,*
> *chances are you'll think that I'm in love with*
> *you."*

I could hear Johnny Mathis singing in my head.

I later teased him that I had only said "yes" to his proposal because he took me out to eat in restaurants, and that was the only time I got a decent meal.

At home, I didn't like to use Mrs. Batey's cooker. One time after work, so as not to disturb her, I toasted a crumpet on a toasting fork held in front of the electric fire in the sitting room. Unfortunately, the crumpet fell off the fork and stuck to the bars of the electric fire. I was unable to retrieve it before it stuck to the metal guard and burned. I had tried to clean it off, but Mrs. Batey wasn't amused, so I decided not to try that again!

Brian told me I was an accident waiting to happen, and it certainly seemed that way. So, while he was home, I made sure that he treated me to as many restaurant meals as possible. One day Brian picked me up for a date and said, "Would you like to meet my Mum?"

I looked at him with an enquiring look. "But I have already met her," I said, thinking of Nell.

"No, she's not my mother; she is my step-mother. My parents are divorced."

I looked at him in amazement. I had never heard of, or met, anyone who was divorced before.

"I thought that only happened in America," I said to him.

So, he took me to meet her. Gert (short for Gertrude) was tall, smart and very welcoming. She was the daughter of an Army Sergeant Major and was brought up in India. Brian was so like her. Gert's husband Mac was Scottish and very funny, and they had a daughter called Alison. I took to them all straight away.

We shared the news of our engagement and, although they were happy for us, Brian's mother said that she would not be coming to our wedding, so as not to cause any trouble with the family. She knew that Nell didn't think much of her, and she didn't want to embarrass us, and spoil our special day. I felt that this was very thoughtful of her, but I know Brian would have loved for her to come. However, it was not to be.

Brian's lovely and charming step-sister Lindsay, Nell's daughter, lived with her husband, Maurice, in Village Way in Beckenham. They had a charming three-bedroom semi. One day she said to me, "If you'd like to, when you are married, you can live with us until you find your own place. You can have the back bedroom and back sitting room, if you don't mind sharing the bathroom and kitchen with us." I mentioned it to Brian, and he was pleased that this was how we could begin our married life.

We both got on well with Lindsay and her husband. Maurice had agreed to be Brian's best man. So it was decided.

While planning for our special day, I learned that Brian was born a Roman Catholic. I assumed that he would want me to become Catholic too. When I spoke to him about this, he replied, "I haven't been to church for years, and I don't believe in it, so I don't mind what religion you are, or what church we get married in." He went on to suggest that we get married at St. Margaret's Church on Plumstead Common.

I agreed, though looking back if we had chosen the little old St. Mary's Church in Bexley, that had a Lychgate at the entrance, it would have made a lovely backdrop for our wedding photos. However, we went to see the Vicar of St. Margaret's. He said he would not marry us, as I had not been baptized.

Having been born during the Second World War, being baptized was not one of the things high on my parent's list of things to do. With the world around us going mad, churches seemed to be concentrating more on funerals than baptisms. It was important for me to be married in a church, so we decided that I could still be baptized, even if it was a little late. The Vicar agreed that he would baptize me on Brian's next leave, then he would be happy to marry us.

Then Brian was gone again, back to New Zealand, but this time he would be sailing on the Southern Cross. He would be due back in November, but I wished he would be home sooner. As I daydreamed about him, this popular song came to mind.

> *"I don't need sunny skies for things I have to do*
> *It's raining in my heart cos I can't be with you*
> *I'm only waiting till the day you're home to stay*
> *So it might as well rain until September.*
>
> *My friends look forward to their picnics on the beach*
> *Yes everybody loves the summertime*
> *But, Oh my darling while your arms are out of reach*
> *The summer isn't any friend of mine..."*

26

OPERATION THELMA

It was October 1961 and Thelma had been complaining about the pain in her feet for some time. Her feet were even worse than mine, with both big toes crossed over onto the other toes. She had gone to see the doctor, and now the date of her surgery appointment at the hospital had arrived. She would be having her operation in Joyce Green Hospital – the same Hospital where Daddy had passed away.

At the hospital, we made our way to the Orthopedic Ward. It bought back memories of the last time we came to visit Daddy together. "Look, its Ward 14!" I said to Thelma. The same number as our flat and our house - that's got to be lucky!" She brightened up as I gave her a kiss and a hug, and left her to get settled in as I made my lonely way home.

After Thelma had her operation, I went back to visit her, bringing flowers. I walked into the long ward where the beds stood side by side along the walls, each with identical coverlets. The nurse pointed Thelma's bed out to me at the far end. When Thelma saw me, her face broke into a smile, mixed with pain.

"Hello, how are you?" I asked as I took her hand. Thelma was anxious to show me how she was, and as she removed the bed covers and protective cradle, I was shocked to see that both feet were encased in Plaster-of-Paris from her knees to her toes. On the sole of each foot was a long ski-like structure. The toe end of this 'ski' stretched beyond her toe. Each ski had five wires coming from it, each of which pierced the top of each one of her toes to straighten them. Thelma told me that they had also cut into her calves to tighten the muscles effectively, pulling her toes straight.

It looked like Chinese torture to me, and she was obviously in a lot of pain. It was hard to think of something to say to cheer her up. After about half an hour, the nurse approached with some more painkillers, so I put the flowers in water, kissed her and left. Poor Thelma!

Eventually, when she was able to come home, she delighted in showing us her new straight toes. The scars on her legs were still quite visible, but we were told that they would soon fade. It was so lovely to have her back at home with me again. I had felt quite lost without her.

In the meantime, I had received many letters from Brian, from all over the world. I had also paid several visits to Jack and Nell and his stepsister, Lyndsay. They had all taken good care of me while Thelma was in hospital, by feeding me and allowing me to stopover. One time I even slept in Brian's bed, and somehow it bought him closer. Lyndsay and I had a hilarious time trying to do my laundry in Nell's washing machine. She wasn't any more skilled with machinery then me.

It was January 1962, and the skiing holiday that I had been planning with Kathleen had arrived. A month before, we went to dry ski school in London to get our muscles accustomed to the exercise, and now we were all ready for our trip. We were to be flying out of Heathrow in a DC6 airplane. I was very excited. I had never been on an aircraft before.

We embarked the plane, found our assigned seats, and sat down. Struggling with my seatbelt, it became very clear to me that my belt was broken and wouldn't fasten. So, I held onto the arm of the seat as the plane began to taxi down the runway. "Please, God, keep us safe," I said under my breath feeling mounting alarm. We picked up speed and were about to take off when the plane suddenly dropped back to earth. Over the intercom, the pilot informed us that he was unable to take off, and that we would all have to go back to the terminal. We were ferried back and then spent hours waiting to see what would happen. Finally, at two a.m., they told us that we would not be flying out that night, and that they had arranged for us stay at the Ariel Hotel for the night.

So after collecting our luggage, we were taken to the hotel. After a restless night, we were woken to a quick breakfast and then steered toward a coach that would take us back to the airport.

Happily, once aboard the plane again, I checked my seatbelt. It worked. I was so tired from the late-night that I promptly fell asleep. I was awoken with a start by the loud voice of the Captain, announcing that we were coming into land. I suddenly felt nauseous and quickly found the sick bag, just before I threw up. This was too much excitement for my stomach. Although we had missed a day of our holiday, we were happy to finally go out onto the snowy peaks and try out our moves.

Between skiing and eating, I wrote to Brian about the wonderful time we were having. I described the delicious apres-ski food, hot chocolate and cream cakes. I told him about the evening get-togethers with the English teaching the Austrians the 'Hokey Kokey' (you put your left leg in…) and about the Austrians entertaining the British with their thigh-slapping Tyrolean dances.

One day Kathleen and I decided to go for a walk to visit the different shrines that were dotted along the road. The snow was coming down in large feathery flakes, so we built a snowman and then went for a walk along a mountain path. I can't begin to describe the beautiful scenery with the snow on the trees; it seemed like another world.

Every turn in the road brought a different scene onto which we would feast our eyes. One side of the road was a steep drop, and the other side the mountain face, and every so often, we passed huge icicles hanging from the rocks. If you looked closely, you would see green leaves and moss perfectly preserved within the icicles.

On our walk, at one point, the road became so narrow that we would have to jump out of the way of approaching vehicles only to land almost up to our thighs in deep snowdrifts. It was a huge laugh. Every so often we passed a beautiful shrine with flowers and greenery placed underneath.

All the time, it was snowing huge flakes. I'm sure we looked like walking snowmen, with the snow clinging to our eyebrows and lashes. We stayed quite warm, and when we turned back, we started singing all the rousing songs we knew at the tops of our voices. As we approached Solden, we could hear the church bells ringing across the valley. I don't think I shall ever forget that day. It was truly magical!

On the day that we were to return to England, there was a snowstorm. Kathleen and I, again, sat in the airport awaiting our flight. Two pilots were seated behind us, and I heard one say to the other, “I don’t fancy flying in this.” Well, that was comforting, I thought. However, we did fly in the snowstorm and, I’m happy to say, we landed safely. Kathleen and I breathed a huge sigh of relief as we taxied to the terminal. It had been a wonderful holiday.

27

SHEILA RETURNS

It was May 1962, and after discovering another dance venue, Crayford Town Hall, Thelma and I went dancing there one Saturday night. This particular night I learned a new dance called 'The Creep,' where you and your partner held hands with your other hand at your side. We took two steps forward and one back. Looking back at this, it has become yet another transient dance craze that emerged from the sixties, like the 'Hand Jive', the 'Twist,' and the 'Mashed Potato,' to name just a few.

It was at this dance that Thelma met a young man called Roy Gregory. He was very tall and thin. I thought that he seemed very nice. Thelma told me proudly that Roy had been in the Guards. Well, he certainly had the height for it! Roy was engaged to be married to another, but one look at Thelma, and it was love at first sight. He broke off his engagement and started dating Thelma instead.

Roy was so keen to get to know Thelma. After the dance, he spent ages looking through the phone book for her phone number. As soon as he found it, he phoned and said he was coming round to take her out.

At this point, I no longer went dancing with them as I didn't want to play 'gooseberry.' So, as Thelma continued dating Roy, I was beginning to feel lonely. Now I started to understand how Thelma must have felt, looking after Daddy and the boys while I was gadding about. So, I began to write more letters to Brian and eagerly awaited letters from him. His letters were always full of news and of how much he loved me, and missed me, and would sometimes arrive three at a time.

Sheila and Ron decided to come back to the south to sell our house on Pelham Road. They were to be living in the house while they sorted out the real estate details.

Thelma, Roy and I went round to our old house to visit them, and to announce Thelma and Roy's good news. We shared how they had known each other for just fifteen days, and he had asked her to marry him, and she said, "Yes!"

Sheila's youngest son, Adrian, was talking a lot now and his latest saying was "poor me." He sounded so funny, he also kept saying, "help me!" He would sit on David's lap and pull David's face into strange expressions, and then attempt to make the same faces himself. Young Adrian took to Roy as well, another good point in Roy's favour. Sheila and I liked him for the way he cared for Thelma.

On the work front, the Agency had found me a job I might like, and I went for an interview. I landed the job with Warner Pathe in London. I was to be working in their records department, keeping records of all the films rented out to the Cinemas right across the Country.

I was sharing an office with two men, a girl about my age, and an older woman. Everyone was very friendly, and I started to enjoy my work at last. The girl, Margaret, and I were able to go to lunch together, and we found some excellent restaurants along the road from the office. The older woman, Mrs. Crisp, had a son who was a cartoonist. She was also very artistic and sketched terrific pictures. She used to come and chat with me, and she made me feel welcome.

One day Thelma phoned me at the office and told me that if I could get away for the afternoon, Roy was going to take us both for a drive. He was bringing a friend so that we could make up a foursome. As luck would have it, my boss was in a good mood and agreed, so Roy, his friend and Thelma picked me up from the station and we drove to Margate.

On the way, we flew along the road with radio Luxembourg blaring, each of us singing at the tops of our voices. We went into the amusement park, 'Dreamland,' and had a great time on all the rides. Then we went for a meal and finally drove back, arriving home at two in the morning, worn out but happy.

It was now September 1962, and Thelma was about to be married to Roy. I was to be bridesmaid together with Thelma's best friend Barbara. As Brian would be back home at that time, Roy asked him to be his Best Man.

On cloud nine, I travelled down to Southampton, where Brian met me at the Station, and we fell into each other's arms. It was so wonderful to be with him again. He took me back to see his ship, the Southern Cross, and I was allowed to board and have a look around. The ship was huge, like a floating hotel. The Captain was holding a children's party on board for children who were born disabled when their mothers had taken the drug Thalidomide while they were pregnant. It was so sad to see these little ones without limbs, and I was very moved.

Brian collected his things from his cabin. He was leaving the Southern Cross for good now because he had been promoted to the status of 'First Electrical Engineer,' and was to join another ship. We caught the train back to London and went back to his place.

We were both so happy that Brian had decided to join the Coptic, a ship that would be sailing around the coast and only going as far as Antwerp, so we would no longer have to be apart for three months at a time.

Brian on the Coptic 1960

Thelma's wedding plans were under way. Thelma, naturally, was to make her own Wedding dress and all the bridesmaids dresses. She had bought some cream brocade from John Lewis in Oxford Street, for her dress. The bridesmaids would be wearing a pretty peach coloured taffeta, with satin shoes dyed to match. It was such an exciting time. I loved my dress and couldn't wait to wear it.

We arranged a 'hen night' for Thelma and decided to go to the new Chinese Restaurant in Dartford. I hadn't had Chinese food before this, as it was a new concept for our area. Thelma had also invited my friends Sylvia, Sybil, Anne and Evelyn, together with Barbara, another bridesmaid and her other friends from Hides. It was a real 'girly' evening with lots of laughing, giggling and jokes. The food was terrific, and we all agreed it was the best hen night that we had been to. Well, it was the only hen night I had been to.

Thelma's Wedding Day passed in a daze. There was some rain, and at one point, after the ceremony, I was concerned to see Thelma crying. She was so overcome with it all and broke down from all the excitement.

The newly-weds spent a two-week honeymoon together in the West Country, and then Thelma and Roy returned to the pub in Dartford that they had bought and which they were to run successfully together.

Thelma also did some dressmaking to keep her hand in, and to make some extra money.

I was living in Mrs. Batey's bungalow on my own now, Brian had returned to the sea, but as I had my wedding to look forward to it wasn't so bad. I was counting the days till Brian came home and we could be married.

We were able to phone each other more now as he was only going around the coast of the United Kingdom. The furthest place he was going to was Glasgow, and we were writing to each other so frequently now, it almost made up for not being able to see and be with each other. Each letter I received made me love him more. I felt so lucky to have found a man like him, so kind, thoughtful and generous, and what is more, he loved me!

Planning our wedding seemed to bring Brian closer to me. I wished that Daddy could have met him. I am sure they would have got along so well together and that Daddy would have approved of my choice of a husband. I also wished that Daddy could have given me away, but as that was not to be, I was hoping that my brother Brian would do the honours. I sent a letter to ask him if he would. I received a reply to say that Val was now pregnant with her second child and it was due about the time of my wedding. He thought it best not to leave her on her own, so he declined.

I didn't know what to do. I consulted Thelma. "Well, it will just have to be David." She exclaimed. Well, that was all right with me, but I wondered how David would feel about it. David seemed more grown-up now, and since we no longer lived together, we seemed closer.

When I asked him, he smiled and said, "That would be great!" He was pleased that I had asked him. So that problem was solved.

I was twenty-four now, and I very much wanted to be married to Brian and start our life together. My landlady, Mrs. Batey enjoyed us spending time together. We were getting on quite well and one day she told me, "You know, even if you are engaged, you can still change your mind, you don't have to go through with it."

I smiled. There was no way I was going to change my mind. But it was kind of her to advise me, I thought. Brian now was, and always would be, the love of my life. We were to be married in December.

> *"To know, know, know him*
> *Is to love, love, love him*
> *Just to see him smile*
> *Makes my life worthwhile*
> *To know, know, know him,*
> *Is to love, love, love him*
> *And I do."*

Often, I would visit Thelma and Roy at their flat over the pub, and sometimes stay overnight. Thelma and I would have lots of fun planning for my wedding. As I was to be having a winter wedding, we chose a satin dress, trimmed with white swan's down, giving the effect of fur. My dress would be slim fitting with long sleeves and a train. I had chosen to have three nieces as bridesmaids, just like Thelma's wedding. I chose Sheila's eldest daughter, Janet, to be one of my bridesmaids, with two of Betty's girls, Doreen, and Joyce, and Janet's brother, Stephen, to be a pageboy. Lindsay, Brian's stepsister, would make a great matron of honour. Nell offered to make some of the bridesmaid's dresses and Stephen's trousers. We learned later that she had a lot of problems fitting Lindsay for her dress. Her measurements changed at each fitting, and Nell couldn't understand why, until Lindsay revealed that she was pregnant.

Lindsay had a beautiful singing voice and I had wanted her to sing a solo in the church. But she declined because she felt she would be too conspicuous with her ever-increasing waistline. At least, she still wanted to go ahead with being my matron of honour, so I was thankful for that.

On a Saturday in October, Thelma and I got on a train and travelled to London to buy the material for my wedding dress and for the bridesmaids' dresses. We went to John Lewis in Oxford Street because the fabric department was massive! What a choice there was, I had never seen so many different fabrics.

We found the ivory Duchesse satin for my dress; it cost only seven pounds and 10 shillings, ($14.50c.) I chose a lovely, deep blue velvet for the bridesmaids' dresses and page boy's trousers. The sleeves and the young bridesmaids' ha-los would both be trimmed with soft white swan's down.

Thelma then took me into D.H. Evans to choose my headdress. She told me that I could borrow her veil, so I only needed the headdress. I would rather have had a long veil, but we had decided that Thelma's veil would be my 'something borrowed.' So that meant we didn't need to buy another one.

I gazed around at the beautiful floral headdresses and tiaras. My gaze finally fell onto a tiny satin one. It was like a small crown with a latticework of diamantes, and little pearl drops standing up all around the edge. I fell in love with it. "That's the one I want," I said, pointing to the glass case. The assistant helped me try it on with Thelma's veil, which we had brought with us. I loved it and felt like a princess, gazing at myself in the mirror. "That will look perfect with your satin dress," Thelma said enthusiastically. So, it was decided, and we waited anxiously while the assistant wrapped it carefully in white tissue paper, placing it in a large box with the D.H Evans logo all over it. Before we caught the train home, Thelma treated me to tea and cakes at Lyon's corner house by Charing Cross Station. The whole trip had been so much fun and a resounding success!

The next thing to think about was the wedding flowers. As I had decided that my bridesmaids would wear a circlet of swan's down and carry matching blue velvet muffs, there would be only flowers to plan for were two bouquets, one for Lindsay and one for me, the groom's and best man's buttonholes, and guest's corsages. I discovered a florist who worked from home, so I went to see her. As I poured over her floral design catalogues, I could picture it all coming together. For my bouquet, I decided upon an all-white, straight shower bouquet of roses, freesia, stephanotis and lily-of-the-valley, with a smaller version for Lindsay. As I paid the florist, I left her a piece of the blue velvet fabric so that she could match the ribbon, and I went home with my spirits high.

28

OUR WEDDING

THREE WEEKS BEFORE OUR WEDDING, BRIAN ARRIVED HOME. WE had made arrangements to visit St. Margaret's church for my baptism. We stood around the baptismal font with just Thelma and Roy, as witnesses. Brian became my Godfather that day, which felt a little strange, but I was so glad that he had agreed to do that for me.

My work colleagues at Warner Brothers had arranged a collection for me, and with the money, my friend Mrs. Crisp helped me choose a wedding gift. I fell in love with a beautiful coffee set consisting of six tiny coffee cups and saucers and a tall coffee pot. It was gorgeous with a pattern of iris and butterflies on the coffee pot and the saucers, while the cups and lid of the coffee pot were of a deep blue. It would be perfect for after-dinner coffee. There was enough money left to buy a little cream vanity case to go with the suitcase I had received from my friends at Anglo American. It would be perfect for taking away on Honeymoon with me. I was thrilled with my choices.

The day before I left work to get married, Mrs. Crisp handed me a long box containing something she had made for me. "It's a garter," she explained as I opened the box, puzzled. Inside was a blue satin garter trimmed with cream coloured lace, and she had written the date of our wedding on the back.

"It's your something blue," she explained. I thanked her and hugged her. She was a very kind and thoughtful lady.

It was foggy on the day before the wedding. Thelma had planned a hen night for me and decided that we would go to the same Chinese restaurant where we attended her hen night. Brian was to go out with all the men for his Stag night. It was such a happy evening for both of us.

After a most enjoyable meal, Thelma, Lindsay and I had arrived back at Thelma and Roy's place when we heard the men coming home. "Quick," said Thelma, to me "Brian is here, and it is unlucky for him to see you before the wedding." So, I hid in the next room, listening to a drunken Brian banging on the door and shouting, "Let me see my wife!" I felt a little worried and wondered what I had got myself into, but there was no way that would I come out of the room.

In the end, Roy persuaded Brian to leave, and Maurice took him back to his own house to sleep it off. Goodness knows what Brian had been drinking. Thankfully it was the first, and last time I would ever see him in this state. (Except that I hadn't seen him.)

After the coast was clear, I came out of the room. Lindsay and I said goodbye to Thelma, as Roy offered to drive us back to Horsham Road in the now increasing fog. Remembering the foggy night of the Lewisham train crash, I sent up a silent prayer for our safety. The fog was not quite as bad as that night, but it was pretty bad all the same.

We arrived safely back at the bungalow, relieved that we had arrived in one piece. Lindsay would be spending the night with me at my home because, as my maid of honour, she would help me get ready for my wedding. We said goodbye to Roy as he left for a hair-raising drive back to Dartford. Thankfully he arrived there safely too.

I went to sleep, worried that our wedding day would be foggy. When I awoke the sun was streaming in through the window.

I had anticipated that I would be in a daze on my wedding day, so I had written myself a schedule of all the things I had to do so that I would forget nothing. Lindsay found my notebook and read it out loud:

- Have a bath
- Put on makeup
- Put on perfume

"Do you think that you would forget to do those things?" She asked me, laughing.

I smiled rather sheepishly. "It's just that I want everything to be perfect and for nothing to go wrong." I explained.

Just then, the flowers arrived. As I looked at them, I noticed that the blue ribbon didn't quite match the bridesmaid dresses, so I decided to do without it and cut it all out. The bouquets were quite beautiful without decoration, and the stephanotis and lily-of-the-valley had a lovely heady perfume that filled the room.

As I got ready, I gazed at my wedding dress hanging on a hanger from the top of the wardrobe door; it looked so beautiful. Thelma had given me countless fittings, and her sewing, as always, was exquisite. Lindsay looked lovely in her dress. She was attaching my veil to the headdress, to put it on my head when David arrived in a car driven by Roy.

David, was coming to give me away, and Mrs. Batey and Lindsay left with Roy. Lindsay took her bouquet and the buttonholes to join the other bridesmaids at Pelham Road, as they would all be leaving together.

I finished dressing and walked to the living room where David was waiting. He looked up as I swept into the living room, holding my skirt up. "Well, what do you think. Will I do?"

His face told me what I wanted to know, and as my brother looked out of the window, he announced,

"Madam, your car has arrived." Perfect timing. Brian had hired an Austin Princess to take us to the church.

Just before we left, David took a photo of me standing in the porch of Mrs. Batey's bungalow and as he did that, a black cat walked across the path. Well, what a good luck omen!

David and I got into the car and we started our journey to St. Margaret's Church in Plumstead. People smiled at me as the car passed them. I smiled back at them; I was so happy. Being a Saturday, the Broadway was busy with traffic and shoppers, so much so, that we arrived fifteen minutes late at the church.

At the church, Lyndsay, the other bridesmaids, and our page boy were patiently waiting at the entrance to accompany me up the aisle. The photographer quickly took some more photos.

David placed my hand on his arm, Lyndsay and the children lined up behind us, and we walked up the aisle to the 'Wedding March.'

Our friends and family were there, but I only had eyes for the man standing ahead of me. My handsome husband-to-be, dressed in a dark blue suit with a double carnation in his lapel. As I walked towards him, he turned and saw me. His face lit up. I smiled through my veil.

Later, Brian confessed that when I didn't arrive on time, he was worried I had changed my mind, especially after the incident the night before.

We knelt on the cassocks before the alter. I thought of Mummy and Daddy and imagined them smiling down on us. We recorded the audio of the wedding ceremony.

"Brian John, do you take Wendy Judith …..?"

"I do."

Brian said it so loud he made me jump. Then,

"Wendy Judith, do you take Brian John……?"

I answered, "I do," but in such a shy, tiny voice that no-one heard me. Sadly, I was not heard on the recording either. Thelma told me later that, as she didn't hear me, she thought I had changed my mind too!

The ceremony continued. "What God has joined together, let no man take asunder."

And, just like that, we were finally man and wife!

Brian and Wendy married

When we came out of the Church together, despite the fog the day before, the sun shone down on us.Brian noticed something on the path, he bent down and picked up. It was a small black plastic cat. He handed it to me. Another one, that HAD to be lucky!

The day whizzed by with me in a haze. The reception was at a hall in Eltham. The caterers did us proud serving champagne and a roast chicken dinner. It was a sit-down affair. Later that afternoon, Nell and her sister prepared a buffet for us, and very good it was too. Brian's next-door neighbour and his band of muscians played our tune "Moon River," for our first dance. After that, it was time for Brian and I to cut our cake. There were three tiers in the shape of a heart, decorated with silver cherubs. Everybody loved it.

The reception

For my going away clothes, I wore a red Stewart tartan, short-sleeved, woollen dress under a bright red Corduroy velvet coat, and a beige pillbox faux-fur hat, like the one Jackie Kennedy wore. We were so happy at the end of the day as we waved to everyone from the car, which was driven by Thelma's husband Roy, complete with peaked cap, as he wanted to look like a real chauffeur.

Wendy in her 'going away' clothes 1962

We were to be spending our first night together at the Ariel Hotel, near London Airport (the same Hotel Kathleen and I had stayed at when we flew to Austria). He drove us to the Hotel and held open the doors for us, taking his new role very seriously. He even carried our suitcases into the foyer, touched his cap, and was gone.

At the hotel, Brian signed the register. He was in as much of a daze as I was, he couldn't remember my name, and as I watched, he signed me in as Judy. I said nothing, but waited till we reached our room, and then I turned to face him, "Who's Judy then?" I challenged.

I laughed as he looked shocked and then was so apologetic. He then caught hold of me and wrapped his arms around me. "I love you, Mrs. Appleton," he said, kissing me hard on the mouth. I kissed him back and felt a warm glow as I knew that nothing, ever again, would be anywhere near as important as the love we had for each other. When we finally made love for the very first time, we knew that we had undoubtedly found true love. I was so glad that we had waited for this, for now, it was so very special. At last, we could be together forever!

The next day we flew to Jersey for our Honeymoon.

Now, after all these years and many ups and downs, we have reached our 57th Anniversary. We still feel the same about each other as when we first met. We are still very much in love, maybe more so. One day I shall tell you the story of our life together as man and wife, and the many twists and turns that finally brought us to Canada. I thank God for finding me such a wonderful husband and for blessing us with such a beautiful marriage.

ABOUT THE AUTHOR

Wendy Appleton grew up in Kent, known as the 'Garden of England.' Now a great-grandmother, she writes about her memories and adventures in extraordinary detail. Her amusing and delightful writing style draws you in as if you were right there with her. This is Wendy's second book. Her first book, 'A Little Girl's War,' describes life on the Home Front in 1944 when she was five years old.

ALSO BY WENDY APPLETON

A Little Girl's War

Amberley Publishing

ISBN 978-1-4456-0639-2

Printed in Great Britain
by Amazon

72626012R00158